Letters the New York Times Did Not Print

Letters the New York Times Did Not Print

Roger Carasso

To the memory of Francis D. Wormuth

ISBN: 1515228274
ISBN 13: 9781515228271

Table of Contents

Preface

I HAVE SENT MANY HUNDREDS of letters to the *New York Times* "letters to the editor" in response to front-section articles in that newspaper. Over the last ten years or so, it has printed about one every three years, and not necessarily the better ones. What prompted these letters was the desire to expose and combat various hypocrisies and injustices systemic in our political life—for example, phony euphemisms such as "pro-life" instead of antichoice on abortion; "voter integrity" instead of voter suppression; "free speech" instead of drowning the political process in big money; "populist" instead of rightist pseudopopulists; or the international defense of "democracy" instead of championing free market capitalism and oligarchy, the latter two often being confused or equated with democracy. There were daily causes for my critiques of disrespect for facts and truth—or serious omissions—hence the many letters.

I begin this compilation with "taboo" letters on subjects the major media would not touch with a hundred-foot pole. That's our informal censorship. But they are only a sample. Though my letters are responses to *New York Times* articles, those original articles have not been included for three reasons: to save space; they have typically been discarded; and my letters are pretty much self-explanatory. Where they are not, I preface them with some commentary.

It might be helpful to start with the appendix. Part one gives background information on domestic matters with an emphasis on economics; the second part deals with international issues. The letters are arranged by topic and alphabetically (except for the first topic, taboo)—and chronologically within each topic.

The great majority of the letters are supposed to be limited to 150 words, more or less, as required by the *New York Times*, which leaves much unsaid. However, there are four op-ed letters that are much longer—and similarly not printed.

Some topics of importance—like climate change, the National Rifle Association (NRA), racism, and LGBT rights—have been omitted or given little attention because *New York Times* coverage of these topics has not been too defective.

If there is one underlying theme, it is the attack on democracy spearheaded by the Republican Party and abetted by a complaisant rightist Supreme Court. This theme assumes the dominant role of giant corporations and obscenely wealthy individuals. Evidence of this will find some repetition in the letters.

Taboo Topics

THERE ARE CERTAIN TOPICS THAT the mainstream media, including the *New York Times*, will not touch. Among them are events concerning our aggression or interventions in Cuba, Haiti, Rwanda, Vietnam, and Cambodia. Domestically, the major taboo subject is socialism. The letters below were an attempt to remedy these lacunae.

FOREIGN INTERVENTIONS

CUBA

re: Julie Hirschfeld Davis, "Announcing Embassy Deal, Obama Declares 'New Chapter' in Cuba Ties," July 2, 2015.

Hypocrisy 101

Leading Republicans denounced the impending establishment of official diplomatic relations with Cuba. House Speaker John Boehner, for example, asserted that no deals with Cuba should be made "until Cubans enjoy freedom." Who would guess from their comments that Cuba has been the victim for decades of an unlawful, crippling embargo and still ongoing aggression. After all, Cuba did not invade and occupy Florida, but the United States does occupy Guantanamo Bay. The demand for liberty and democracy could provide a standard text for

Hypocrisy 101. The Republicans are trying to prevent women from owning their own bodies. They have eliminated universal suffrage. They're destroying labor unions, long a bulwark of democracy. They have transformed the "rule of the people" into the "rule of money." Then, they have the nerve to proclaim their devotion to democracy, at home and abroad, including Cuba.

re: Randal C. Archibold, "Inequality Becomes More Visible in Cuba as the Economy Shifts," February 25, 2015.

As Cuba allows more private enterprises to flourish, so does inequality start to flourish. That's not surprising, since capitalism requires inequality. Adam Smith even wrote in *The Wealth of Nations* that for every wealthy person, there must be five hundred poor ones. This places capitalism in conflict with democracy, which requires equality. This is Cuba's dilemma. It needs to open up, but opening up can eventually lead not to democracy but to the Kochlocracy that looms so large in American society.

re: Editorial, "Mr. Obama's Historic Move on Cuba," December 18, 2014.

The restoration of diplomatic relations with Cuba is a major step forward. The next major step should be the repeal of the economic embargo, which you suggest restrains the president because of "an outmoded 1996 law," presumably the obnoxious (to Europeans and others) Burton-Helms Act. But it's not that simple. As chief executive, the president is bound to enforce not only domestic laws but treaties as well, which, according to Article VI of the Constitution, are part of the supreme law of the land. The embargo clearly violates ratified treaties, including the Charter of the Organization of American States and the UN Charter. If there are doubts about the latter, one need only refer to the 188–2 vote of the UN General Assembly condemning the embargo, which is clearly identified as violating the charter and international law. Faced with two contradictory laws that cannot both be enforced, the president should have the latitude to end the unlawful embargo.

re: Peter Baker, "US Will Restore Full Relations with Cuba, Erasing a Last Trace of Cold War Hostility," December 18, 2014.

As can be expected, leading Republicans—including Jeb Bush, Senator Marco Rubio, House Speaker John Boehner, and Senate Majority Leader-to-be Mitch McConnell—condemned normalizing relations with Cuba. They hide behind demanding democracy and human rights for the Cuban people. The hypocrisy is sickening. Is such concern for the Cuban people credible, when Republicans are befouling democracy and human rights here at home? Democracy and human rights require universal suffrage, which the Republicans are doing their best to dismantle. Democracy needs strong working classes and labor unions, which the Republicans want to destroy. Democracy is opposed to the rule of billionaires, which Republicans champion. Democracy is incompatible with racism, which they coddle. Democracy requires women's rights; wherever they don't exist, neither does democracy. Yet Republicans are scuttling these rights by undermining the right to contraception and abortion. It's hard to believe they give a hoot for the rights of the Cuban people, while dismantling the rights of Americans. What really horrifies them is Cuban universal medical care—and a society not ruled by Koch brother types. That's what they dread at home.

re: Joe Nocera, "Obama's Gitmo Problem," May 25, 2013.

As Joe Nocera notes, President Obama declared on Thursday that denying the prisoners at Guantanamo due process has made the prison "a symbol around the world for an America that flouts the rule of law." Neither Obama nor Nocera, however, mentioned violations of treaties such as the UN Charter, the Rio Treaty (1947), or the Charter of the OAS (1948), all of which forbid aggression against other countries—which includes Cuba, whose territory of Guantanamo is being occupied by the United States. Even if the 1903 coerced treaty granting us that base had once been valid, we have nullified it by violating its provision that the base be used exclusively for coaling or naval stations, which precludes building prisons there. To complete our lawless record, we violate even our own constitution, whose Article VI proclaims treaties as part of the supreme law of the land.

re: Damien Cave, "Easing in Cuba Renews Debate on US Embargo," November 20, 2012.

It's time we renounce our imperialism toward Cuba as expressed by our embargo and nonrecognition of the Cuban government. The official reason for our hostility is the desire for democracy and liberty for the Cuban people. This could be convincing only to those unaware of our history. For one thing, we have recognized and armed countries much more repressive than Cuba, including Haiti, Chile, and Guatemala. Secondly, we have a long record of seeking to make Cuba part of the United States since President Jefferson expressed this interest. More directly, President Polk offered Spain $100 million for Cuba. President Pierce in 1854 offered $130 million, and, just before going to war, President McKinley upped the offer to three hundred million dollars—all refused by Spain. We still seem to think Cuba—or at least its fate—belong to us. It's time we shed our vicious and vindictive policy toward Cuba and nourish a belated dose of honesty concerning our foreign policy.

Haiti

re: Frances Robles, "Haitian Leader's Power Grows as Scandals Swirl," March 17, 2015.

The United States refused to recognize Haiti until 1862. It occupied Haiti for nineteen years (1915–1934) and supported the terror-wielding Duvalier regimes (1957–1986). When, with Bertrand Aristide, Haiti finally got a president who cared for his people, the United States had him ousted in 2004. Aristide had democratically won 92 percent of the vote in 2000, with over 60 percent participation. The United States prevented him from coming back to contest the fraudulent elections of 2010, which required a runoff between the two top candidates. The United States saw to it that one of them was disqualified so that Michel Martelly could be in the runoff, though he gathered only 4 percent of the total votes. Naturally, Martelly won the March 2011 runoff elections (with less than 17 percent of the electorate) and continued the prowealthy, probusiness, corrupt regime that the United States typically favors. Martelly has in effect dissolved Congress and has virtually no checks on his rule and corruption. That's our man!

re: Randal C. Archibold, "Jean-Claude Duvalier 1951–2014, Second-Generation Haiti Dictator Known as Brutal 'Baby Doc,'" October 5, 2014.

The United States has a long history, especially in Latin America, of supporting elites or oligarchs, and suppressing populist movements and governments. Haiti is one tragic example. The long obituary of brutal Haiti dictator "Baby Doc" Duvalier, a good friend of the United States, casually mentions that populist Jean-Bertrand Aristide—whose party, Fanmi Lavalas, won a majority in every election in which it was allowed to participate—"was chased from the country by political upheaval." How innocent sounding, especially with the omission that the United States supported the 2004 coup that ousted Mr. Aristide, and even kidnapped him to Africa. The United States prevented Aristide from returning to Haiti before the 2011 presidential elections, so that our favorite, Michel Martelly, could win through crooked means we supported. Martelly, a good friend of Baby Doc and Haitian elites, mourned Baby Doc's passing. No wonder his regime is highly popular with US authorities.

re: Editorial, "Haiti's Long Road," January 2, 2013.

There is a more basic reason than those mentioned in your editorial why Haiti is far from repairing the damages inflicted by the dreadful 2010 earthquake, despite pledges of billions of dollars in foreign aid. The major reason is that for decades, including the present one, Haiti has been governed by terror (for example, Tonton Macoutes), dictatorship, drug criminals, corrupt politicians, army and business elites, all of which could have cared less for the ordinary Haitian people. The exceptions were the brief rule of Jean-Bertrand Aristide, elected with 67 percent of the vote for his first term in 1991 (overthrown by a military coup the same year) and his second term, elected in 2000 with over 90 percent of the vote, which was also ended in 2004 with a military coup supported by the United States. He was the only Haitian leader who cared about the masses, their education, housing, and health—and was therefore anathema to the US-supported upper classes. Now that things are back to "normal," the Haitian people can expect continued suffering.

RWANDA

re: Editorial, "After Rwanda's Genocide," April, 9, 2014.

Your editorial mentions "unanswered questions" and the "shameful paralysis" of the United States during the Rwandan genocide. But it carefully avoids unanswered questions about the role of our protégé, Paul Kagame, in his invasion of Rwanda in 1990 at the head of the displaced Tutsi aristocrats, with Ugandan help and US encouragement. It does not mention the mass murders that followed this invasion. It does not mention what part Paul Kagame and the CIA had in the assassination of Rwanda's president, Juvenal Habyarimana, in 1994—which sparked the reactive Rwandan genocide. Nor does it ask about Kagame's later contribution to millions of Congolese deaths.

It may turn out the problem was not insufficient US involvement, but rather excessive involvement, in what produced the Rwandan horrors.

re: Alan Cowell, "Twenty Years After, Rwanda Pauses to Recall Carnage," April 8, 2014.

The United States excels at causing horrors, then with feigned innocence, expressing outrage. It violated promises not to expand NATO eastward after the collapse of the Soviet Union, then proceeded to expand the alliance right up to Russia's frontiers. Russia reacted by annexing Crimea, to our indignation.

Earlier, we had expressed horror at the Rwandan genocide, discreetly veiling what had provoked it: our support of Paul Kagame when he invaded Rwanda (with Ugandan support), caused massacres, then assassinated Rwanda's president, Juvenal Habyarimana, in 1994—which led to the reactive genocide. Kagame as Rwandan President was later implicated in the deaths of millions of Congolese. In the 1970s, we organized rightist General Lon Nol's overthrow of neutralist Prince Sihanouk in Cambodia. Lon Nol's unpopularity led to the take-over by the Khmer Rouge—and the "killing fields," which piously outraged us. Our compliant media cooperated by not mentioning these unpleasant realities. The present article is a good example.

re: Alissa J. Rubin and Maia de la Baume, "France to Shun Genocide Services After Rwanda Leader Fixes Share of Blame," April 7, 2014.

It is no wonder a French judge accused Paul Kagame of complicity in the assassination of Rwandan President Juvenal Habyarimana in 1994—most likely with CIA support. Kagame had earlier—with Ugandan and US encouragement—invaded Rwanda to try to restore the overthrown Tutsi aristocracy. He initiated massacres that led the Hutu government to seek more UN observers—which the United States and Great Britain blocked. Kagame's actions were the catalyst for the Hutu reaction, the notorious genocide that ended when Kagame's troops conquered Rwanda and Kagame was made president. Kagame then intervened in the Congo, which contributed to millions of deaths. However, a wall of silence here has fallen over his actions, probably because he was an instrument of US policy.

re: Helene Cooper, "UN Ambassador Faulted for Rwanda Tie in Congolese Violence," December 10, 2012.

US Ambassador to the United Nations Susan Rice's hobnobbing with and protecting Rwanda's President Paul Kagame, who enabled M23 to wreak mass murders, rapes, and terror on the hapless Congo, is shameful. But it's not the first time the United States has been involved in mass murder involving Rwanda's Kagame. The press has given copious coverage of the Hutu's genocide in Rwanda. However, it has neglected mentioning how the Clinton administration winked at Kagame's assassination of Hutu President Juvenal Habyarimana in April of 1994—or that, allied with Ugandan troops and continued US support, Kagame's minority Tutsis invaded Rwanda, caused mass murders, and ignited the retaliatory genocide by the majority Hutus. The United States did its best to prevent UN observers from witnessing Kagame's atrocities. Rwanda is a serious blot on our record.

Vietnam And Cambodia

re: Sheryl Gay Stolberg, "Pentagon's Web Timeline Brings Back Vietnam and Protesters," October 10, 2014.

The Pentagon is planning a fiftieth anniversary commemoration of the Vietnam War, which will supposedly "provide the American public with historically accurate materials." I doubt this will include the following truths.

1) The Geneva Accords of 1954, which ended the French Indo-Chinese War, provided that Vietnam should be neutral and not part of either the Soviet or American bloc. We immediately violated that by setting up SEATO (Southeast Asia Treaty Organization) to cover South Vietnam.
2) The Geneva Accords provided for reunification of both Vietnams by 1956 through elections, elections we successfully sabotaged. President Eisenhower's memoirs (*Mandate for Change, 1953-1956*) admitted that the communist leader Ho Chi Minh was hugely popular and would have won.
3) Our invasion of Vietnam was an act of aggression prohibited by numerous treaties, including the UN Charter. It resulted in roughly one-tenth of the Vietnamese population dying.

4) We bombed Cambodia furiously, oversaw the overthrow of Prince Sihanouk, which eventually led to the Khmer Rouge take-over and the "killing fields" of Cambodia, with more millions dying.
5) Many have acknowledged that the war was a "mistake." It was far worse. It was a horrendous crime.

Maybe it's appropriate to celebrate our soldiers—or Nazi soldiers or communist soldiers, or any soldiers. But that should not blind us to what we have done.

How Much Longer Can We Perpetuate Our Lies about Vietnam? August 21, 2004.

The Swift Boat Veterans for Truth's second ad attacks John Kerry's 1971 Senate testimony in which he mentioned war crimes in Vietnam. That ad (unlike the more easily discredited first ad slandering Kerry's decorated battle service) is harder to refute, some Democrats admitted privately, because it deals with Vietnam veterans' personal feelings of betrayal from such testimony. ("Kerry Is Filing a Complaint against Swift Boat Group," August 21, 2004). What makes the ad effective is that this nation is continuing to live a lie about what Vietnam stood for. Five hundred thousand-plus foreign troops from a giant power trying to impose its will on a defiant small country is classic imperialism. This was a war against not just a small army but against the whole people, or at least 80 percent of them (the number President Eisenhower estimated would have voted for the communist patriot Ho Chi Minh). This was the kind of guerilla war that virtually compels atrocities. As long as we subscribe to the myth that our intentions are always honorable—which would be a miraculous historical first for any great power—that we intervened to help the Vietnamese people, and that we were in no way involved in a brutal and devastating war of aggression, we perpetuate a lie pervading our entire political discourse and permitting the character assassination of men like President Clinton and Senator Kerry.

How long our national life will remain poisoned by lies about Vietnam—and Cuba, for that matter—is the issue here that must be addressed. A life of denial will eventually catch up with any individual; and so it will with our country. 9/11 is one more warning about that.

Domestic—Socialism

Please note: part of the bottom paragraph was added; it came from a second (and shortened) submission to the *New York Times*.

re: Editor, *New York Times* Op-Ed, June 21, 2015.

THIS IS THE TIME TO TAKE A LOOK AT SOCIALISM (THE GOLDEN RULE)

With democratic-socialist Bernie Sanders running for the presidency, this is a good time to take a new look at socialism (the golden rule)—even though the senator's platform is more New Deal than socialist. However, a similar devotion to justice animates both. Americans have been taught to dread the words "communism" and "socialism." Partly this is due to the crimes of Stalin's Soviet Union. Some of these crimes were due to the encirclement of the Soviet Union by hostile forces, part of them were due to Stalin's paranoia, power obsessions, and lack of moral scruples. Though there were socialistic aspects to the Soviet Union, (for example, free education and health care), it is a serious and constant mistake to view Stalin's "communism" as genuine socialism. Would it be fair to blame Jesus for the horrors inflicted by "Christian" nations who invaded, colonized, robbed, tortured, and murdered millions of inhabitants in less-developed societies—while plunging the world into two global wars, and the Holocaust? It would be no fairer to blame Karl Marx for "communist" atrocities.

Socialism is a socioeconomic system where the major economic assets, including the means of production, are communally owned, and the economy is managed for the common good, rather than for the selfish interests of dominant classes. Marx envisaged a future communist society where the underlying principle would be, "From each according to his ability, to each according to his needs." This is exactly the same formula underlying the first Christian community, as described by the New Testament: "Nor was there anyone among them in want. For those who owned lands or houses would sell them and bring the price of what they sold and lay it at the feet of the apostles, and distribution was made to each, according as any one had need" (Acts of the Apostles 4:34–35).

But what does this have to do with the Golden Rule? Everything, since the rule is at the heart of socialism. The rule has had universal appeal. Do unto others as you would have them do to you, said Jesus (Luke 6:31). Rabbi Hillel declared, "That which is hateful to you, do not do to your fellow. This is the whole Torah; the rest is commentary." When asked if there is "one word that can serve as a principle of conduct for life," Confucius replied, "It is the word *shu*—reciprocity. Do not do to others what you do not want them to do to you." (Analects 15:23). The rule is found in Buddhism, Hinduism, and even in the ancient Egyptian Book of the Dead. The social application of this rule is socialism. If you want adequate wealth, a good home, safe neighborhoods with good schools, good health care, etc. for yourself, this is what you should strive for with your neighbors or fellow citizens. If you don't want to be subject to dominant classes, then you shouldn't try to subject others to your rule. It is those principles that make the Golden Rule applicable—and would be maximized in a democratic socialist country.

What is the alternative? Today's global capitalism. Undoubtedly, capitalism has remarkable achievements. Its technological innovations have been spectacular. It has brought multimillions into the middle class, especially in India and China more recently. Nevertheless, it is a world full of injustice, corruption, and violence.

The United States, for example, seems to be in perpetual wars. According to the Stockholm International Peace Research Institute (SIPRI), in 2014, the United States alone accounted for over one-third of total global military expenditures. Though for a couple of decades following World War II, the United States had an enormous middle class, this is changing rapidly as the richest 1 percent increasingly accumulates at the expense of the lesser classes. One reason was the decapitation of unions, which had served to enlarge the middle classes. Though some one-third of workers had been unionized in the 1960s, by today the total has shrunk to barely over 10 percent. Technology and globalization were major causes for this steep decline. In 1965, the income ratio of the CEOs of the top 350 firms to that of their workers was 20:1. By 2014, it had mushroomed to 296:1. The richest 400 people in 2014, according to the Forbes 400, had an aggregate net worth of $2.29 trillion. The wealthiest 0.1 percent (not 1 percent but 0.1 percent—some 166,000 families) held 22 percent of America's wealth. Whereas a huge majority of Americans considered themselves "middle class" in the 1950s, the number had shrunk to 60 percent in 2005, and 51 percent in 2015, according to a Gallup poll.

White-collar criminals who destroy the environment, like Duke Energy, get a slap on the wrist. Even billions of fines levied against giant banks, like Citibank or JP Morgan Chase, for criminal activities hardly disconcert them while, of course, their executives stay out of prison. Wall Street, which nearly brought down the economy in 2008, continues essentially the same practices unfazed. Even the scientific community is involved in cheating: "Cheating in scientific and academic papers is a long-standing problem, but it is hard to read recent headlines and not conclude that it has gotten worse" (*New York Times*, June 1, 2015). As Jean-Jacques Rousseau wrote, "When profit is the only goal, it is always more profitable to be a rascal than an honest man" (*Considerations on the Government in Poland*). Perhaps worse is the **legal** corruption involved in buying elections, buying public officials (executive and legislative at both the federal and state level—and judges in some of the states), and buying legislation by hordes of lobbyists. Income taxes for the wealthiest have withered, from 90 percent in the 1950s to 39 percent today. Corporate taxes accounted for 33 percent of total federal revenues in the 1950s now shoulder only 9 percent. The burdens have of course been shifted to the middle and lower classes. Not surprisingly, there is little faith in politics. A 2014 Gallup poll revealed that only 7 percent of respondents had confidence in Congress; 29 percent in the presidency. It's no wonder that today 65 percent think the country is on the wrong track, versus 28 percent who think it on the right track (*Rasmussen Reports*, "Right Direction or Wrong Track," June 1, 2015).

It's not that things are better in the rest of the world. *Share the World's Resources* (STWR) reported in 2011 that almost half the world lives on less than two dollars a day. "An average of 50,000 people die of poverty each day, or 18 million each year." The World Bank (Poverty Overview 2015) stressed progress but still saw over 2 billion people living on less than two dollars a day (a "common measurement of deep deprivation"). In the meantime, according to OXFAM, the richest 80 persons (80, not 80,000) in 2014 held as much wealth as did the 3.6 billion poorest people, or half the human species! And then there's global corruption that infects nearly all countries, especially in Africa, Asia, and Latin America. Even the most important and glamorous sports association in the world, FIFA (Fédération Internationale de Football Association), saw several of its top executives criminally indicted in 2015. There's also brutal and criminal human trafficking. A 2014 Global Report on Trafficking in Persons found at least 152 countries of origin and 124 countries of destination. The US Department of State (Trafficking in Persons Report 2014) estimates over 20 million victims of trafficking have not even been identified in the past year. Millions are forced to live as slaves.

In the meantime, wars rage in the capitalist world. World War I caused some 20 million deaths; World War II, nearly 60 million. Some 10 percent of the Vietnamese population died as a result of the American invasion. A 2008 report by the International Rescue Committee (IRC) estimated that 5.4 million Congolese had died of war-related causes between 1998 and 2007. In the 1990s, Indonesia wiped out up to one-quarter of East Timor's population.

The Middle East is on fire. Some five hundred thousand casualties were inflicted on Iraq by the American intervention. At least two hundred thousand have died in Syria since 2011. I'm not saying that capitalist interests, as such, caused all these wars, but rather that the context for all these wars was a capitalist global economy.

Finally, there are the environmental planetary disasters involved in climate change, which is caused largely by human actions. President Obama and the Pentagon now view it as the greatest national security threat. Droughts will bring on dramatic upheavals, with population dislocations—and even water wars. One could argue that drought is what brought about the present Syrian civil wars. Melting Arctic and Antarctic ice will produce not only rising temperatures in the oceans (with harmful climate changes) but also the flooding of various coastal areas. Capitalist profits have prevented any effective action in curbing it. Pope Francis's encyclical *Laudato si'* condemned a "structurally perverse" market economy, exploiting the poor and turning the earth into an "immense pile of filth." Climate change, just by itself, is a good reason to take a second look at socialism. If socialism doesn't make an appearance in the foreseeable future, it may well be too late for adequate life on this planet.

Capitalism

re: Danny Hakim, "US Chamber Travels the World, Fighting Curbs on Smoking," July 1, 2015.

The heart and soul of capitalism is to make profits. That is the sole purpose of capital. For such an economic system, "morality" means profits; "immorality" means financial losses. Therefore, it is hardly surprising to read that overseas branches of the US Chamber of Commerce are devoted to fighting restrictions on smoking, that is restriction on profits. Yes, tobacco kills, but that is not relevant to capital, unless financial losses are involved. Oil and gas companies are perfectly willing—for the sake of immediate profits—to imperil the planet and the human species. The total subordination of life and death to profits is the hallmark of capitalism—and a very good reason to consider a totally different economic system, like socialism, devoted to welfare for all, rather than profits for the few.

re: David Brooks, "The Democratic Tea Party," June 16, 2015.

David Brooks can't understand Democrats opposing the proposed Trans-Pacific Partnership trade deal when similar deals, like NAFTA, have produced so much prosperity abroad. Naturally he doesn't mention who prospered.

It's true Vietnam raised its average hourly minimum wage to just over one dollar in 2014. Bangladesh had a nine-cent hourly minimum wage; India, twenty-five cents; Indonesia, fifty cents—and Mexico, which supposedly is luxuriating, raised its hourly minimum wage to sixty-five cents in 2015. The world was so well off in 2011 that nearly half its population lived on less than two dollars a day, with an average of fifty thousand people dying of poverty each year. Most recently, some eighty individuals owned as much as half of humanity, according to OXFAM. We know who prospered, and it certainly was not the American worker, whose plight is obviously of no concern to prosperous Mr. Brooks.

re: Thomas L. Friedman, "Democracy Is in Recession," February 18, 2015.

Thomas L. Friedman rightly holds up Tayyip Erdogan's increasingly authoritarian Turkey as a symbol of deteriorating global democracy. He concedes that political deadlock in America is involved in the erosion of democratic "self-confidence." What he (and virtually no one else) doesn't mention is the incompatibility of capitalism with democracy. Democracy stands for equality; capitalism for inequality. Democracy stands for liberty of individuals; capitalism for "free markets." Democracy values human beings as such; capitalism values them only as workers, farmers, entrepreneurs, etc. When the Koch brothers can announce nearly one billion dollars in planned electoral contributions, there goes democracy. Can anyone really believe democracy is possible in a world where eighty— eighty!—individuals own as much as 3.5 billion people, that is, half the entire human species. All our ideologies cannot erase these realities.

re: Steven Rattner, "Europe's Anti-Business Stance," January 29, 2015.

Wall Street financier Steven Rattner bewails Europe's "archaic restrictions on hiring and firing workers." He's also upset over wages rising in France and

Italy without accompanying worker productivity. He says nothing about great increases in worker productivity in the United States NOT accompanied by wage raises. He's also unhappy with Germany's promoting of clean power. On the other hand, he's very pleased with Spain, which is making it easier to fire workers, though he admits a 24 percent unemployment rate there. He doesn't mention that over half of those under twenty-five years of age are unemployed or that Spain had to borrow heavily. What Rattner really seems to want is ending any New Deal type of humanity and the downward march of wages to the Bangladesh level. Europe's social conscience stands in the way of this, but not financier Rattner's conscience or lack of it.

re: Kenan Malik, "Radical Islam, Nihilist Rage," January 4, 2015.

Kenan Malik got it right in noting that the Islamic State—Boko Haram, the Shabah, the Taliban, etc.—expresses an anti-imperialist hostility to globalization. Our foreign policy universally and unfailingly supports the wealthy upper classes against the less-privileged classes. This is a magnet for discontent and rage. Socialism having been wiped out, the remaining outlet is Jihad. Benjamin Barber (*Jihad vs. McWorld*) sees the world as divided between Jihad ("driven by parochial hatreds," a "rabid response to imperialism") and McWorld (which universalizes markets and societies through ruthless multinational corporations). Each reinforces the other and imperils democracy. It is a choice between homogenized individuals and fanatic ones. It is a tragic choice that begs for a third, though unlikely, alternative like democratic socialism.

re: Erich Schmitt, "In Battle to Defang ISIS, US Targets Its Psychology," December 29, 2014.

The military brass and other government leaders are having a difficult time understanding the magnetizing force of ISIS, which inspires so many volunteers. Maybe one reason is, as Upton Sinclair wrote, "It is difficult to get a man to understand something, when his salary depends on his not understanding it." Our foreign policy universally and unfailingly supports the wealthy upper classes against the less-privileged classes. That is a magnet for discontent that we cannot afford to understand, at least publicly. Benjamin Barber (*Jihad vs. McWorld*) sees the world as divided between Jihad ("driven by parochial hatreds," a "rabid response to imperialism") and McWorld (which universalizes markets through ruthless multinational corporations), both of which require the other and both of which disregard liberty, while seeking to dismantle democracy. It's not all that difficult to understand, though harder to acknowledge.

re: N.R. Kleinfield, "A Vast Sea of Blue, Mourning the First of Two Slain Comrades," December 28, 2014.

More than twenty thousand police officers came to the funeral of Officer Rafael Ramos, murdered on December 20, along with another officer. NYC Mayor de Blasio, NY Governor Cuomo, and even Vice-President Biden attended. This outpouring would not, of course, occur for ordinary victims. The reason is symbolic. The police have a dual function. To maintain the peace, and to enforce the property and class structure of the society. It is the latter function that was being celebrated indirectly, because the preservation of society is no small matter. Adam Smith in *The Wealth of Nations* wrote, "For one very rich man there must be at least five hundred poor," and it was the function of the state to maintain this class and property structure. In 2013, millionaires numbered 9.63 million, including 490 billionaires. That requires a lot of poverty—and a heavy police force to keep it that way. It's that crucial, unmentioned police function that drew such a national display of mourning.

re: Douglas Dalby, "Immigrants Are Increasingly Met with Fists," November 19, 2014.
Steven Erlanger, "British Premier Plans Tougher Stance as Anti-Immigration Sentiment Grows," November 19, 2014.

Sebnem Arsu, "In Turkey, Francis Advocates Dialogue in Battling 'Fanaticism,'" November 19, 2014.
Ibrahim Garba Shuaibu, "Fatal Attack Causes Chaos at a Mosque in Nigeria," November 19, 2014.

Fanaticism and terrorism do not come from nowhere. They are the expression of poverty, alienation, and various dislocations. The annual UN High Commissioner for Refugees (UNHCR) estimated there were over fifty million refugees in 2013. The murderous civil wars in the Middle East, Africa, and elsewhere all have something in common. They all come from a world dominated by capitalism. That world has seen the most war casualties in history: forty to eight-five million in World War II; fifteen to sixty-five million in World War I; twenty to one hundred million in China's Taiping Rebellion (1851–1864); and many millions more in the recent Congo and Sudanese wars. Between 1870 and 2001, the frequency of wars increased by an average of 2 percent yearly. The eighty-five richest people alone own as much as the poorest half of humanity, reported OXFAM. Then there's the destruction of the environment and planet earth's species. This is the world that capitalism has wrought.

re: Nicholas Confessore, "Outside Groups with Deep Pockets Lift GOP," November 6, 2014.
Jonathan Martin, "In States Seen to Be Tilting Left, Voters Defy Democrats' Forecast," November 6, 2014.

Big Money and Karl Marx Win

Big money is a huge part of the Republican midterm landslide victories. Voters were angry about Washington being "broken." So whom do they vote for? The obstructionist Republicans who broke it. That's what big—and often secret—money and propaganda can do. Voters were soured by an economy that benefited primarily billionaires and multimillionaires. So whom do they vote for? Obstructionist Republicans who prevented a healthier recovery that would benefit nonbillionaires. That's what big money can do. President Obama and Democrats enabled millions of their fellow citizens to get health care and live longer. What happened? Giving millions their first access to real health care becomes a crime, and not a virtue. That's what big money can do. Voters really, actually believe that, with the Republicans in power, they will get beneficial change. In short, that old devil Karl Marx had it right. Whoever controls the economy controls both the political system and the minds of citizens. When the Democrats win, that control is only some 80 percent. When the Republicans win, it soars to the upper 90 percent.

re: Frank Bruni, "Capitalism's Suffocating Music," October 22, 2014.

Frank Bruni writes that only one of the major league baseball stadiums had a corporate moniker twenty years ago. Today, twenty of the thirty stadiums are named for corporations. Everything is being commercialized. It's "capitalism run amok." "Hucksterism," he wrote, "invades everything, scooping up everyone." Many Americans are alienated by the tax and other privileges accorded to the wealthy, on top of this universal commercialism. We might as well face it—we have become a plutocracy with some remaining democratic elements. One promising remedy is to return to a New Deal type of capitalism with a government having a strong social conscience. This would require the Republican Party to develop a social conscience, something highly unlikely. The other promising remedy is to forge a democratic socialism, which is even more unlikely given the control of the media and government by the wealthy. We're drunk on capitalism, and until it crashes, there won't be a twelve-step healing process toward socialism.

re: Monica Davey, Bill Vlasic, and Mary Williams Walsh, "Detroit Ruling Lifts a Shield on Pensions," December 4, 2013.
Mary Williams Walsh, "Pension Ruling in Detroit Echoes West to California," December 4, 2013.

Rick Lyman, "Illinois Legislature Approves Retiree Benefit Cuts in Troubled Pension System," December 4, 2013.
Eduardo Porter, "Americanized Labor Policy Is Spreading to Europe," December 4, 2013.

The "Idolatry of Money" Continues Unabated

In his apostolic exhortation, "The Joy of the Gospel," Pope Francis condemned the "new tyranny" of unfettered capitalism, growing inequality, and the "idolatry of money." Today's news illustrates dramatically what the pope condemned. A federal judge made an unprecedented attack on public pension rights, concerning Detroit's bankruptcy hearing. But it's a ruling that could spread "West to California" (Mary Williams Walsh), permitting nationwide assaults on hitherto protected pension rights, as is happening now in Illinois (Rick Lyman). This illustrates the growing war on the middle classes as the rich keep getting wealthier. Europe, which had sought to protect working class standards and benefits, now finds itself following the American path of hammering working-class benefits ever downward (Eduardo Porter). The news, coming a day after the papal exhortation, seems as if it's intended to validate Francis's condemnation of the global economic system.

re: Michael Cooper, "Your Ad Here, on a Fire Truck? Broke Cities Sell Naming Rights," June 25, 2012.

The New Feudalism and the Dying Democracy

With private wealth accumulating in plutocratic coffers, while the public goes broke, we're seeing an acceleration of privatization. Domestically, this involves advertisements on public transit systems or recreation centers, administering the profitable parts of public parks, the running of prisons, transferring public schools to charter schools, or creating private residential enclaves with their own governors. If Republicans had their way, it would also extend to the postal service, social security, Medicaid, and Medicare. Internationally, by 2006, about 70 percent of government expenditures on foreign and domestic intelligence were outsourced to contractors. In the 1991 Gulf War, the United States employed one private contract worker for every 100 American soldiers. In early 2011, there were more private contract workers than US soldiers in Iraq. In early 2012 in Afghanistan, there were more private contractors' employees than US soldiers. Private armies fight in Somalia or are hired by Arab sheikdoms. Add to this the penetration and control of governments by corporate titans, and we get New Feudalism, where private wealth (land ownership in feudal times) conferred political or governmental power on corporate (feudal) lords. This spells the end of democracy, which can't come soon enough for the billionaire Koch brothers and the Roberts Supreme Court.

Climate Change

re: Rick Gladstone and Somini Sengupta, "Site of ISIS Vandalism Ranks among the World's Most Important for Archaeologists," March 7, 2015.

Islamic State fighters are continuing their depredations. Shortly after having burned down a library in Mosul, Iraq, and destroyed three-thousand-year-old artworks and priceless antiquities, ISIS has vandalized the ancient city of Nimrud, using sledgehammers and bulldozers to destroy irreplaceable antiquities. UNESCO's director general, Irina Bokova, condemned "the systematic destruction of humanity's ancient heritage." Other violent Islamic extremists contributed their own similar vandalism, for example, the Taliban's destruction of the giant Bamiyan Buddhas, or Wahhabi Islamic extremists in Timbuktu, Mali, who demolished centuries-old Sufi shrines and mosques. Unfortunately, this vandalism of the human mind and art is matched by the corporate vandalism of climate and nature, which threatens the lives of the human species. Both vandalisms must be stopped.

re: Helene Cooper and Jane Perlez, "US Flies Over a Chinese Project at Sea, and Beijing Objects," May 23, 2015.

The Chinese are dredging the contested Spratly Islands (claimed by at least three other countries) in reclamation projects to convert small reefs into islands capable of holding ports, bases, and recreation centers. To show its objection, the Obama administration is flying observation planes over areas the Chinese claim as their territory. Those are just pinpricks. The really effective answer is given by those shrewd Republicans who deny climate change and thereby serve to accelerate it. It's just a question of time before these artificial islands get flooded (along with many areas like Miami) and rendered inoperative. The Chinese have finally met their match.

re: Coral Davenport, "In Climate Deal, Obama May Set a Theme for 2016," November 13, 2014.

China and the United States have agreed on steps to limit climate change, including for the United States, reducing carbon emissions 26 to 28 percent by 2025—while China pledged to stop emissions growth by 2030 if not sooner, while producing 20 percent of its energy from renewable sources. Republicans, who had used previous Chinese abstention to reject curbs on US production, were thereby deprived of a major issue. This did not stop major Republican leaders like Senator Mitch McConnell or Speaker John Boehner from denouncing the agreement. The likely Republican presidential candidates have already denied climate change. Ignorance, or feigned ignorance, is the Republican trump card. Republicans rely on an electorate that doesn't believe in evolution. They typically display contempt for facts or scientific opinion. The reign of ignorance naturally favors the growing role of big money and oligarchs. It's unfortunate that Republicans don't seem to care for their grandchildren. Or perhaps they believe that an elite can escape the ravages of climate change. Too bad for the rest of us.

Democrats

re: Jonathan Weisman, "House Democrats Spurn Obama, Endangering Trade Pact," June 13, 2015.
Peter Baker and Jennifer Steinhauer, "In Defeat, a Divide for Obama and His Party," June 13, 2015.

House Democrats overwhelmingly rejected an aspect of the Trans-Pacific Partnership (TPP), thereby damaging a Republican objective, strangely supported by President Obama. Republicans made it a priority to block all of Obama's proposals—unless, as with TPP, these benefited billionaires and multinationals. Was it as the president of a capitalist society, or as an occasionally naive president, that Obama championed the TPP? In his *Audacity of Hope*, Obama naively wants a partnership with Republicans. It took him years to discover the GOP was more interested in torpedoing him. Now, Obama naively (?) claims that the TPP is good for American workers and the country. If it were really so, why would the Republicans back it? Their only primary desire has consistently been for what benefits the wealthy, and that doesn't include workers. The big corporations sucked in President Obama, but he couldn't suck in his Democratic party.

re: Amy Chozick, "Clinton Says GOP Rivals Try to Stop Young and Minority Voters," June 5, 2015.

Hillary Clinton singled out Governors Rick Perry, Chris Christie, and Scott Walker for their efforts to disenfranchise voters, especially the young and minorities. She mocked their rationale of "a phantom epidemic of election fraud." Indeed, Loyola University professor Justin Levitt, an expert on elections, showed there were only thirty-one credible incidents of voter impersonation out of one billion ballots cast from 2000 to 2014. Clinton criticized the Republican Supreme Court for gutting the 1965 Voting Rights Act, thereby permitting much more voter suppression. Since universal suffrage is essential to democracy, she asked, "What part of democracy are they afraid of?" Unfortunately, the answer is "the whole of democracy itself." This is why the Republicans are turning the rule of the people into the rule of the wealthy, to accompany voter suppression.

re: William Neuman, "Obama Hands Venezuelan Leader a Cause to Stir Support," March 23, 2015.

The United States has a long history of hostility toward leftist regimes, that is, regimes not devoted primarily to helping its upper classes. It has tried, usually successfully, to overthrow them. Examples include Cuba, Haiti, Chile, Grenada, Guatemala, Honduras, and Nicaragua. Reestablishing diplomatic relations with Cuba seemed to signal a change. However, President Obama has recently—and absurdly—designated Venezuela as an "extraordinary threat to the national security" of the United States. He didn't specify what IBMs with hydrogen bombs Venezuela was about to launch against this country—perhaps because it doesn't have any. He also inflicted some sanctions against several Venezuelan officials, something bound to help President Maduro, who readily recalled blatant US interventions in Latin America. In terms of vindictive nonsense, this is on par with registering Cuba as a terrorist state.

re: Editorial, "Lessons of the James Risen Case," January 22, 2015.

The *Times* is right that the Justice Department's attempt to subpoena reporter James Risen to compel him to reveal sources and testify in the trial of former

CIA officer James Sterling was part of a worrisome tendency of that department to harass reporters of leaks. The Obama administration has brought more leak cases than all previous administrations combined. An important lesson is clearly to enact better federal shield laws to protect reporters. Another important lesson, omitted by the *Times*, is the hypocrisy of the rightist Roberts Supreme Court. For years, that court has invoked phony free speech/First Amendment rights to protect big money polluting the political process. But when a genuine First Amendment case arose with James Risen, the court turned it down (*Risen v. the United States*, 2014). That court deserves much more scrutiny and less good-faith assumptions.

re: Motoko Rich, "Push to Add Charter Schools Hangs Over Strike," September 13, 2012.

The Republican War on Democracy

The Republicans have waged a three-pronged attack on democracy: (1) the war on women, (2) the war on universal suffrage, and (3) the war on labor unions. The last, unfortunately, has received substantial Democratic support concerning teachers' unions in particular.[Democratic Chicago mayor] Rahm Emmanuel's support of nonunionized charter schools is a prime example. There are trillions, not mere billions, to be made by privatizing the public schools. The respectable cover is the well-being of school children. If that were serious, we would see a real war against poverty, overcrowding, drugs, crime, violence, and unemployment. It's a shame to see prominent Democrats partially abetting the Republican war on democracy.

A Missed Opportunity for "Free" Medical Coverage—2010

President Obama was correct in rejecting Representative Price's claim that the GOP had advanced proposals that could provide universal coverage "without raising taxes by a penny." There is no way, stated the president, of suddenly covering an additional thirty million people where "it costs nothing." (David M. Herszenhorn, "Searching for Some Light amidst the Heat," January 30, 2010). But in fact, there is a way—of course, not the Republican's way—but rather one suggested by Himmelstein, Woolhandler, and Wolfe in the *International Journal of Health Services* (2004), who pointed out that if the states had adopted, in 2003, a single-payer administrative structure such as Canada's, they would have saved $286 billion dollars, enough not only to cover some forty million uninsured, but with plenty left over to boost the benefits of the underinsured. This is a beauty of a "freebie" which, unfortunately, the president did not have the acumen or courage to snare by championing the extension of Medicare to all Americans.

The Shameless and the Spineless—2014 Op Ed

The Republicans are shameless. What else can you call a party that has repeatedly and publicly declared that its primary objective is not the economy, not national security, not general welfare, but to make sure that millions of their fellow citizens do not get health care—that is, to get rid of the Affordable Care Act. If confirmation is needed, the Republican House of Representatives has voted some sixty times to repeal the Act. A Harvard University study in 2009 estimated that some forty-five thousand Americans died yearly from lack of adequate medical care. No major party in human history has ever publicly declared that kind of shameful primary objective. You would think that the Democrats would leap at the chance to clobber the Republicans on this issue. Instead, most have heaped more or less faint praise on the act, when they were not fleeing from it and President Obama in the 2014 midterm elections. That's spinelessness.

Furthermore, the Republicans, aided by the Roberts Supreme Court, have shamelessly waged war on democracy by drowning elections and the political system in floods of big money, thereby turning the rule of the people (democracy) into the rule of money. Again, you would think the Democrats would confront and hammer this Republican attack on our official democratic values. Yet none has directly called the Republicans on this repudiation of democracy. More spinelessness.

Are the Democrats afraid of annoying the combative Republicans? There's hasn't been much collaboration to lose there. Or are they afraid that, if compelled out of their oligarchic closet, the Republicans will proudly proclaim their rejection of democracy, stop the pretense, and act even more brazenly? After all, when the secretive rightist Koch brothers were outed, they then brazenly declared their intention to give some $900 million to the coming election. If fear is what is motivating the Democrats' silence on these issues, that's just more spinelessness.

So that's the dismal choice of the American electorate: whether to support the shameless or the spineless. The spineless, of course, are less nefarious; nevertheless, the American people deserve a better choice.

De-Regulation And Privatization

re: James Risen and Matthew Rosenberg, "Blackwater's Legacy Goes Beyond Public View," 4-15-15

The convictions of four former Blackwater security guards for wanton shooting deaths in a crowded Baghdad neighborhood has put the issue of privatization on the spotlight. Privatization - under pretexts of cheaper or improved performance - is really designed for neither but, rather, for profit. Though exact figures are hard to find, one indication is that in Afghanistan, some 9,800 American troops are dwarfed by almost 40,000 private contractors. In 2011/12, 8% of prisoners were held privately and for profit. They were often farmed out to jobs, bringing additional profits to their owners. Schools have not escaped this profit motive. Public schools are being starved for funds and teachers and unions are being blamed for any resulting problems. Well over a million students are in charter schools, one-third of which were for profit. The Calf of Gold keeps growing.

re: Editorial, "Drowsy Drivers, Dangerous Highways," 6-14-14

As you wrote, the government estimates that some 13% of truck drivers involved in a crash were over-tired. Nevertheless, the trucking industry is trying to loosen federal regulations on maximum driving times for truckers - even though these regulations are not that rigorous and do permit truckers to drive

11 consecutive hours, with just one 30-minute rest break. The trucking industry claims that regulations lead to more traffic congestion. In a way, they have a point. The more people die in a crash, the less congested traffic will be. If a hundred million Americans could be killed in truck crashes, think how smoothly the traffic would flow! And don't forget the parking benefits

re: Howard Blume, "Teach for America is accused of agenda," 8-5-13

The Republicans/Rightists are masters of euphemisms: anti-choice or anti-women becomes "pro-life"; busting unions and workers' pay becomes "right to work"; voter suppression becomes "vote protection"; and unlimited election funds becomes "free speech." Similarly, destroying teachers' unions and privatizing public schools becomes "school reform." Teach for America, founded by union-busting Michelle Rhee (of dubious test scores), seeks to privatize public schools by transforming them into union-free Charter schools with no teacher job protection. It's no surprise that its biggest private donor is Wal-Mart Stores' The Walton Family Foundation. The war on women, on workers and unions, on democratic elections, and on public schools are all cut from the same Rightist cloth.

re: Marc Chafetz, "Invitation to a Dialogue: Our Regulatory System," 5-29-13

Three examples serve to ridicule the idea that the market self-regulates and that we need less, regulation. They illustrate that the lives and safety of people come second to profits. For years, the tobacco industry tried to debunk cigarette ties to cancer and deaths. Yet, still today, nearly 1/5th of all deaths in the U.S. result from cigarette smoking (according to the CDC - Centers for Disease Control and Prevention). Secondly, we have the fossil fuel industries (led by the Koch brothers) trying to deny climate change. They contribute significantly to over 3 million [global] deaths each year from air pollution (according to a

2012 **Lancet**-published study). What the final costs of climate change will be is incalculable. Finally, we have the deregulation, exemplified by abolishing the Glass-Steagall Act in 1999, contributing enormously to the worse economic crisis since the Great Depression, with accompanying human health and death losses. What we need is stronger, not lesser, regulation resistant to giant lobbying sabotage.

re: Michael Cooper, "Your Ad Here, on a Fire Truck? Broke Cities Sell Naming Rights," 6-25-12

The New Feudalism and the Dying Democracy

With private wealth accumulating in plutocratic coffers, while the public goes broke, we're seeing an acceleration of privatization. Domestically, this involves advertisements on public transit systems or recreation centers, administering the profitable parts of public parks, the running of prisons, transferring public schools to charter schools, or creating private residential enclaves with their own governors. If Republicans had their way, it would also extend to the postal service social security, Medicaid, and Medicare. Internationally, by 2006, about 70% of government expenditures on foreign and domestic intelligence were outsourced to contractors. In the 1991 Gulf War, the U.S. employed one private contract worker for every 100 American soldiers - in early 2011 there were more private contract workers than U.S. soldiers in Iraq. In early 2012 in Afghanistan, there were more private contractors' employees than U.S. soldiers. Private armies fight in Somalia or are hired by Arab sheikdoms. Add to this the penetration and control of governments by corporate titans, and we get the New Feudalism, where private wealth (land ownership in feudal times) conferred political or governmental power on corporate (feudal) lords. This spells the end of democracy, which can't come soon enough for the billionaire Koch brothers and the Roberts Supreme Court.

Drugs

re: Timothy Williams and Tanzina Vega, "A Plan to Cut Costs and Crime: Curb Bias against Ex-Convicts," October 24, 2014.

Conviction for a crime virtually wipes out the chance for employment. Without employment opportunities, a return to criminal activity seems like the only option. Most startling is that an estimated one-third of American adults have been arrested, an incredible statistic. It begs the question, is such a crime-producing society worth preserving, unless it reforms itself?

re: Anahad O'Connor, "Increasing Marijuana Use in High School Reported," December 18, 2013.

The Liquor Industry Threatened by Increased Marijuana Use

The data shows that increasing marijuana use correlates with decreasing alcohol use. The implications of this inverse correlation should not be overlooked. The spearhead of opposition to legalizing marijuana is the alcohol industry and lobby. Marijuana threatens their profits. Unfortunately, they have the ears of the federal government and many state governments who together happily arrest hundreds of thousands of people yearly for mere possession. It's ironic that these vested interests pretend alarm over marijuana causing traffic accidents, when it's well known that alcohol is the major culprit there. But there's hope, as common sense pushes more and more states (twenty so far) toward decriminalizing marijuana.

re: Editorial, "A Saner Approach on Drug Laws," September 2, 2013.

It appears the *New York Times* favors a saner but not a sane approach to drug laws. It applauds the new policy of the Justice Department to tolerate state laws permitting marijuana—but isn't ready to allow the national legalization of marijuana, even though it recognizes that there were eight million arrests between 2001 and 2010 at a cost of two to six billion dollars annually. The Drug Policy Alliance noted last year that a study showed that fewer than 10 percent of those who try marijuana meet the clinical criteria for dependence—compared to 32 percent of tobacco users and 15 percent of alcohol users. Twenty states permit at least medical uses of marijuana, while no claims of medical value have been raised for tobacco or liquor. The major unanswered question about the federal government's policies is whether they are more vicious than idiotic, or more idiotic than vicious. That's not an easy one.

re: Charlie Savage, "Department of Justice Seeks to Curtail Stiff Drug Terms," August 12, 2013.

It's fine that Attorney General Eric Holder wants to curtail stiff drug criminal terms, but that's not nearly enough. First of all, it's absurd to classify marijuana—along with the most dangerous drugs—under Schedule One. It has obvious medical benefits, and twenty states have legalized it for medical purposes. Secondly, drug arrests in 2010 totaled 1.6 million (mostly by state and local authorities) with nearly half being for mere possession of pot. Under his policies, President Obama would have been arrested long ago. The "war on drugs" began with President Nixon and has cost over one trillion dollars by now. It's been a brutal failure that has ruined countless lives unnecessarily. It's time to substitute common sense and humanity for mindless dogmatism.

Education

re: Motoko Rich, "Middle-Class Pay Elusive For Teachers, Report Says," December 3, 2014.

Teachers in less-favorable cities are hard-put to reach a middle-class income and life style. Nationally, the average teacher salary lies somewhere between fifty-five thousand and fifty-six thousand dollars—while the top hedge fund managers averaged over one billion dollars each last year. There's a war against teachers—especially teacher unions and unions generally—that accounts in good part for these low salaries. Fiscal priorities also weigh in, with primacy residing in not taxing and giving tax loopholes to billionaires. Talk about topsy-turvy values in a sick society!

re: David Brooks, "The Unifying Leader," November 25, 2014.

David Brooks plugs the need for a collaborative president, one who would differ from President Obama. One has to wonder how well such a "collaborative leader" would function while facing a party holding a veto on policy—and whose primary declared objective would be to destroy that leader politically. I don't know how much anyone would want to collaborate in his or her own destruction. It's interesting that the only specific example mentioned by Brooks on how such collaboration would work concerns schools. In exchange for increased preschool funding (a Democratic idea), the collaborative leader would grant the Republican wish for charter schools to replace public schools. Wholesale privatization is no compromise. It's the educational Holy Grail of rightist Republicans (and many conservative Democrats). In short, Brooks goes a long way to disguise his primary objective, to enshrine the clout and profits of the wealthy, in the guise of "collaboration."

re: Jennifer Medina, "Teacher Tenure Ruling in California Is Expected to Intensify and Broaden Debate," June 12, 2014.

The Republicans and the rightist Roberts Supreme Court have teamed up to demolish democracy by abolishing universal suffrage, unleashing the floodgates of big money that corrupt elections, undermining abortion rights, and attacking labor unions. The latter issue got a boost from the ruling of Republican (former California Governor Pete Wilson-appointed) judge Rolf M. Treu, who declared teacher tenure unconstitutional. Like his fellow rightist cohorts, Judge Treu hid his real motive by pretending concern for poor and minority students suffering from bad teachers retained by tenure. Of course, if quality education for all were really his concern, he would have lambasted the socio-economic realities that doom these children. As Harvard professor Susan Johnson explained, "It's all in the context of a lack of general support for unions," the pillars of democracy.

re: Motoko Rich, "A Walmart Fortune Spreading Charter Schools," April 26, 2014.

CHARTER SCHOOLS AND THE WAR ON DEMOCRACY

It is useful to analyze important issues in a broader context. That broader context today is the war on democracy, which has two major prongs: transforming the rule of the people into the rule of money, and suppressing voting rights and jettisoning universal suffrage. Both are spearheaded by the rightist Roberts

Supreme Court, the GOP, and allied foundations and billionaires. This is the context necessary to analyze the war on public schools and unions.

Unions are a bulwark of the middle classes and democracy. Dismantling unions is necessary for getting rid of democracy. Charter schools do that, which is why they are backed by hundreds of millions of dollars from the Walmart family and foundations. Their professed "moral obligation to provide families with high-quality choices" (Marc Steinberg, high Walton Family Foundation official) is an ugly joke in the face of starvation wages for unionless Walmart workers. Furthermore, dismantling the public schools can lead to hugely profitable privatization at the expense of the alleged beneficiaries, the students. This is a war we had better understand and take seriously.

re: Dan Frosch, "Resistance to a State's Evaluation of Teachers," December 18, 2013.

New Mexico ranks near bottom by most education metrics. It is also the forty-fifth poorest state in the union. That's the correlation that should be stressed, rather than what most Republicans and some Democrats prefer to stress: teacher inadequacy and the need to rely more on standardized tests. The more relevant correlation resulting from widespread poverty would lead to the sort of soul-searching we prefer to avoid. In its editorial today, the *New York Times* appropriately cites the effort of more successful countries to reduce inequalities in school funding. Poverty and poor education have been historical partners.

It's also useful to look at the overall context—which is the successful war of the 1 percent against the rest of our country. That war requires thrashing the middle and working classes, which in turn requires destroying labor unions. That's what too many of our so-called "reformers" really want, under the guise of helping out "our kids."

re: Howard Blume, "Teach for America Is Accused of Agenda," August 5, 2013.

The Republicans and rightists are masters of euphemisms: antichoice or anti-women becomes "pro-life"; busting unions and workers' pay becomes "right to work"; voter suppression becomes "vote protection"; and unlimited election funds becomes "free speech." Similarly, destroying teachers' unions and privatizing public schools becomes "school reform." Teach for America, founded by union-busting Michelle Rhee (of dubious test scores), seeks to privatize public schools by transforming them into union-free charter schools with no teacher job protection. It's no surprise that its biggest private donor is Walmart Stores' Walton Family Foundation. The war on women, on workers and unions, on democratic elections, and on public schools are all cut from the same rightist cloth.

Re: "Invitation to a Dialogue: A Student's Call to Arms," October 10, 2012.

President Bush's "No Child Left Behind" and President Obama's "Race to the Top" have something in common: a determination not to deal with the basic causes of school deterioration. Nearly all Republicans and many Democrats not only share that commitment, but have also decided that teachers and unions constitute convenient scapegoats. If you're really serious about improving K–12 education, then confront the major problem: poverty. While good teaching can make some difference, it cannot overcome the enormous burden faced by children from neighborhoods ravaged by unemployment, poverty, drugs, crime, and the family dislocations these produce. Naturally, it's easier to blame teachers and invent quantitative criteria than to remedy the enormous inequalities our society engenders.

Foreign Affairs

re: Editorial, "Central America's Migrant Crisis," June 16, 2015.

The editorial recommends focusing on the root causes for so many thousands seeking to flee their homelands in Central America: "gang violence, chronic poverty, high unemployment, and weak government institutions." However, the editorial discreetly omits an even more serious factor: the US historical determination to get rid of any government that really addresses these problems. In Central America, this includes the Nicaraguan Sandinistas we ousted from power. In Honduras, we backed the military coup that overthrew President Manuel Zelaya in 2009—though the coup was overwhelmingly condemned by the United Nations, the OAS, and the European Union. Zelaya's basic crime was raising the minimum wage by 60 percent and caring for ordinary people. Now that country has one of the most unequal distributions of wealth, and two-thirds of its citizens live below the poverty line. That's the sort of thing we publicly deplore, while supporting it.

re: Elisabeth Malkin, "Wave of Protests Spreads to Scandal-Weary Honduras and Guatemala," June 14, 2015.

The Obama administration wants to send one billion dollars in aid to Guatemala, El Salvador, and Honduras to fight gang violence responsible for thousands of children seeking asylum in the United States. There's an irony there in that the gangs sprout from a wretchedly impoverished population—and their corrupt regimes, which we have long supported, including their previous death squads. It's as if we were eager to send firefighters to fight flames that we arsonists created. We had a chance to support a populist, honest regime when it was ousted in Honduras in 2009 by our friends, the military. We quickly acquiesced in the dictatorship, a good example of how serious our global commitment to democracy really is. But what can you expect, when we're getting rid of our own type of democracy here at home.

re: Michael R. Gordon, "Survey Points to Challenges NATO Faces Over Russia," June 10, 2015.

A Pew survey revealed that most Germans, French, and Italians oppose using military force to defend a NATO ally attacked by Russia. Undoubtedly, public opinion there is influenced by the bogus case pressed by the United States concerning Ukraine. The United States virtually compelled a strong Russian reaction to its increasing attempt to encircle Russia with hostile forces, including the projected incorporation of neighboring Ukraine into NATO. Imagine the US response if the Soviet Union's Warsaw Pact had expanded into Mexico and eyed Canada as next. If our hysteria over little Cuba is any indication, we would have invaded Mexico and Canada with massive forces. Only 29 percent of Germans blamed the Russians for violence in Ukraine. It sounds like these European countries are less censored than the United States, where our mass media never mention our provocations and portray Russians simply as aggressive evil-doers.

re: Julie Hirschfeld Davis, "Over Beer, Obama and Merkel Mend Ties and Double Down on Russia," June 8, 2015.

A specialty of the United States is to bewail disasters we cause. One example: US intervention in Cambodia (during the Vietnam War) led to the ousting of

Prince Sihanouk, which led to rightist Lon Nol (1970), which led to his overthrow by the Khmer Rouge and the "killing fields," about which we couldn't caterwaul enough, though it wouldn't have happened if we hadn't intervened. Another example: the Rwandan genocide. What led to it was our backing of Paul Kagame's invasion of Rwanda and murder of Rwanda's president, which is what precipitated the genocide we're still loudly deploring. A more recent example: Despite the warning of Russia expert George F. Kennan, we expanded NATO to Russia's borders, thereby provoking a violent Russian reaction, just as Kennan had predicted. How indignant we were at what we provoked! Let's hope this specialty dies down.

re: Julie Hirschfeld Davis, "Obama Seeks to Reinforce Isolation of Russia," June 7, 2015.

Just before expanding NATO eastward to include Poland, Hungary, and the Czech Republic, the United States got a sober warning from probably its foremost Russia expert, George F. Kennan. The planned expansion would be a "tragedy" reviving the Cold War and provoking Russia into reactions we would deplore. The United States kept expanding NATO to Russia's frontiers, with Ukraine scheduled to be next. In effect, it virtually compelled Russia to react violently, which brought about a predictable show of outrage from the United States and NATO partners. The United States wants to keep economic sanctions on Russia, when it needs it for Iran and Middle East solutions. In any case, there's no point sanctioning and deploring when you get just what you asked for. Next time, we should be wiser in what we ask for, lest we get it again.

re: David Brooks, "Learning from Mistakes," May 19, 2015.

David Brooks would have us believe the 2003 attack on Iraq was a mere "misjudgment" by President Bush, "a case of human fallibility," "a major intelligence failure," and certainly not the "fable" that we were lied into war.

Is Mr. Brooks ignorant of George Bush's former ghostwriter Mickey Herskowitz's assertion that, already in 1999, Bush hoped for an opportunity to invade Iraq. Is he ignorant that President Clinton's chief intelligence adviser Richard A. Clarke had written on September 12, 2001, that President Bush pulled him aside and "testily" asked him to find evidence that Saddam was connected to the terrorist attacks? When he reported there was no such evidence, he was told to "Please update and resubmit." Is Mr. Brooks similarly ignorant that Ambassador Joseph C. Wilson debunked allegations that Niger had sold uranium yellowcake to Iraq? Could he even be ignorant that VP Cheney's Halliburton would reap huge profits from war—or the role of oil in Middle East politics? If he is not that crassly ignorant, then he is being slyly deceptive.

re: Azam Ahmed and Joseph Goldstein, "US Campaign in Afghanistan Surpasses Vow," April 30, 2015.

Under the guise of "training and advising"—which is how President Kennedy got us into the Vietnam War—special operations troops are continuing US military involvement in the Afghan war, after we supposedly ended our military intervention. But we have to keep intervening with airstrike and otherwise, because the Afghans on our side are incapable of facing the Taliban by themselves, despite fourteen years of training. This recalls our "Vietnamization" of the Vietnam War, when our Vietnamese trainees were going to withstand the nationalist and communist Vietnamese forces. Naturally, they collapsed soon after we left. It's predictable that when a corrupt and unpopular government relies on massive foreign intervention to stay afloat, when that intervention ceases, these puppet regimes collapse. History is a pain in the neck for our ambitions.

re: Editorial, "The Case for Aid to Central America," February, 9, 2015.

It's absolutely true that Central America needs help. The one basic need you omitted is a government that cares for its nonwealthy citizens. That's precisely the kind of government we systematically opposed or tried to overthrow. To wit: Guatemala (1954), Cuba (1960 2014), Chile (1973), Nicaragua (1980s), Grenada (1983), Venezuela (1999–), Haiti (2004 and earlier), and Honduras (2009). I'm sure the list is incomplete. You sort of hinted at this when you wrote that Central America "continues to reel from the repercussions of American military intervention in the 1980s." Please excuse my being more explicit and comprehensive.

re: Michael R. Gordon and Eric Schmitt, "US Considers Supplying Arms to Kiev Forces," February 2, 2015.

The Obama administration is reportedly considering more aggressive moves, including supplying additional arms, to the Ukraine. Before we succumb to the predictable applause of the neocons, it's worthwhile considering Thomas Friedman's report (*New York Times*, May 2, 1998) of a phone call he had with George F. Kennan concerning the US Senate's approval of NATO expansion to Hungary, Poland, and the Czech Republic. Kennan, the architect of the successful containment policy toward the Soviet Union and probably the foremost expert on Russia, lambasted the action. "I think it is the beginning of a new Cold War...I think it is a tragic mistake." He added, "Of course there is going to be a bad reaction from Russia, and then [the NATO expanders] will say that we always told you that is how the Russians are." Friedman then deplored "the utter poverty of imagination" such policies entailed. Kennan, unfortunately, was the disregarded prophet.

re: Thomas L. Friedman, "Czar Putin's Next Moves," January 28, 2015.

If there's one thing the United States excels at, it's creating disasters and then affecting enormous indignation, as if we had nothing to do with it. We did this in Cambodia in 1970 when we orchestrated the ousting of neutralist Prince

Sihanouk, which eventually resulted in the Khmer Rouge "killing fields," which we outdid everyone in condemning. As for the Rwandan genocides of the 1990s, they resulted from our backing Paul Kagame's murderous invasion of Rwanda. Naturally, we excelled in indignation. In 1998, George F. Kennan, perhaps the country's foremost expert on Russia, saw the Senate's ratification of NATO's eastward expansion as "a tragic mistake," which will be "the beginning of a new Cold War." This occurred in a phone conversation. NATO has now pushed to Russian frontiers and covets the Ukraine. Who could be more indignant at the Russian reaction than the United States? Thomas Friedman is now comparing Putin's reaction to Hitler. Guess to whom George Kennan made his prophetic phone call in 1998. Why, to no one else than an approving Thomas Friedman himself.

re: Jonathan Weisman and Jeremy W. Peters, "Senate Approves Training and Arming Syrian Rebels," September 19, 2014.

The United States as King Sadim (reverse of Midas)

Whatever King Midas touched turned to gold. What King Sadim (the United States) touches turns to dust. In 1954, we invaded Guatemala to overthrow the Arbenz regime, and the next decades saw hundreds of thousands of deaths. In 1960, we orchestrated the overthrow of Patrice Lumumba in the Congo, which by now has suffered millions (not thousands) of casualties. We devastated Vietnam and Cambodia in the 1960s to 1970s, with millions of casualties there also, including the Cambodian "killing fields." More recently, we invaded Afghanistan, whose corrupt government and fractured society are now ripe for a take-over by the Taliban once we leave. In 2003, we invaded Iraq, which is now most notable for repression, corruption, and an inept military—the result of billions we spent there and our policies. In 2011, we bombed Libya, got rid of Gaddafi, and created chaos. We are now poised to intervene in wretched Syria, with both presidential and congressional approval. God help that country!

re: Brenda Shaffer, "Russia's Next Land Grab," September 10, 2014.

The hypocrisy of NATO toward Russia may be swept under the rug, but it's still there. Mikhail Gorbachev, the last Soviet leader, asserted that former Secretary of State James Baker promised him in 1990, "If you remove your troops and allow unification of Germany in NATO, NATO will not expand one inch to the east." Former Senator Bill Bradley wrote that Baker confirmed the words themselves to him. It's clear the Soviets would not have agreed to German unification otherwise. The Czech Republic, Hungary, and Poland nevertheless were brought into NATO in 1999. Then in 2004, Estonia, Latvia, and Lithuania joined, bringing NATO right into Russia's borders. The attempt to add Georgia and Ukraine to NATO finally brought a furious reaction from a betrayed-feeling Russia. And now, Brenda Shaffer wants America to intervene in the Caucasus as well. As Katrina vanden Heuvel noted, George Kennan, the architect of containment, warned in 1998 that NATO's expansion would usher in a new Cold War. "I think it is a tragic mistake." He was right.

Re: Paul Krugman, "Why We Fight," August 18, 2014.

Paul Krugman argues that for modern nations, even easy war victories don't pay. He mentions that the eventual costs of the Iraq war (including veterans' care) will end up topping one trillion dollars. One answer he gives as to why countries still go to war is that "leaders may not understand the arithmetic." He may be right about the nation as a whole, but seems to overlook the fact that war can be very profitable for certain interests. For example, Halliburton's KBR pocketed profits of $17.2 billion from Iraq war–related revenues just from 2003 to 2006. *USA Today* (March 10, 2013) wrote, "The business of war is profitable." Citing the Stockholm International Peace Research Institute (SIPRI) and 24/7 Wall St., the ten largest war contractors sold over $208 billion of arms and military services in 2011 alone. The US defense budget, it added, splurged from about $312 billion in 2000 to $712 billion in 2011. So Krugman may well be right for the country as a whole, especially its wounded veterans, but not for those companies that flourish in wartime.

re: Anne-Marie Slaughter, "Don't Fight in Iraq and Ignore Syria," June 18, 2014.

Anne-Marie Slaughter chides President Obama for not using force in Syria and Iraq. She probably has never heard of King Sadim (King Midas in reverse) who turns everything he touches into mud. That's a fairly accurate description of American intervention. We intervened in 1953 to overthrow Iranian Premier Mossadegh, and now we have the Ayatollahs. We overthrew the Arbenz regime in 1954, and since then, Guatemala has been a horror story. In 1960, we orchestrated the assassination of Patrice Lumumba; millions of Congolese have since died. We devastated Vietnam and Cambodia and got nothing in return. We supported death-squad regimes in El Salvador and Honduras; today, faced with severe poverty and crime, waves of their desperate people are flooding our borders. We intervened in Libya in 2011 and created a royal mess. And of course, there's the chaos that our 2003 invasion of Iraq caused. Not a record to be repeated.

re: David Brooks, "The Autocracy Challenge," May 30, 2014.

David Brooks harbors the illusion that our foreign policy in the past seventy years was devoted "to extend democracy." Its real devotion was to free markets, not democracy—as witnessed by our hostility to democratically elected regimes critical of free markets, such as Allende in Chile or Chavez in Venezuela. Brooks's confusion is understandable, since it's pervasive here to equate democracy with free markets, even though their fundamentals are in conflict. Democracy sees individuals as ends and promotes liberty through equality. Capitalism sees individuals as economic functions and encourages harsh and huge inequalities. Furthermore, it is weird to view the United States as a champion of democracy internationally, at the very time it is destroying its own democracy—which requires universal suffrage and the rule not of money but of the people. If you need more evidence of this, look at the recent research by scholars Martin Gilens of Princeton University and Benjamin I. Page of Northwestern University.

re: Michiko Kakutani, "Writing of History He Helped to Make," September 14, 2014.

The modern father of political realism (Henry Kissinger's credo) was Machiavelli, who wrote that a ruler needs to be "a great hypocrite and a liar." Kissinger is a perfect example of this precept. As Michiko Kakutani points out, Kissinger in his writings evades the "devastating consequences" of the war he helped prolong in Vietnam. For this alone, he qualifies as a war criminal. Kissinger backed the invasion of Iraq, but it's wrong to associate this with an alleged Wilsonian desire to export democracy. American policy has been to export free markets, not democracy, which it has attacked when critical of free markets. As for President Wilson, himself, he invaded Mexico, Haiti, Cuba, Panama, the Dominican Republic, Nicaragua—and Russia, during and after World War I—essentially to fight populist movements. Kissinger's false dichotomy between political realism and Wilsonian idealism is untenable.

re: Peter Baker, "In Cold War Echo, Obama Strategy Writes Off Putin," April 20, 2014.

We started the first Cold War. President Harry Truman thought the atomic bomb would put a "hammer" on the Soviet Union, whose control of border states he refused to recognize. The 1947 Truman Doctrine asserted the right to international counterrevolution. He was echoing the aspirations voiced by influential magnate Henry Luce (*Time*, *Life*, *Fortune* magazines) who, already in 1941, hailed expectantly "the first great American century." We claimed to be countering Soviet global imperialism, whereas we saw the Soviet Union as blocking our drive for world dominion, which we pretty much achieved. We are also starting the second Cold War by reneging on our promises to Russia by expanding NATO right to its frontiers. Russia dreaded NATO incorporating the Ukraine and reacted. We can no longer rule the world, and we need Russia for troop movements in Afghanistan, nuclear inspections, arms control, and problems with Syria and especially Iran; so there will be limits to this Cold War.

re: Charlie Savage, "President Tests Limits of Power in Syrian Crisis," September 9, 2013.

The powerful never lack scribes to justify their immoral or illegal actions. This applies to the numerous presidential violations of the constitutional provision that only Congress can plunge this country into war. Alexander Hamilton (Federalist Paper #69) made it clear that, unlike the king of England, the president would have no such powers. This has been repeatedly violated since World War II, including alleged "limited types" (Charlie Savage) like Reagan's invasion and occupation of Grenada in 1983. The UN Assembly overwhelmingly (108–9) rejected Jeanne Kirkpatrick's fraudulent explanation that this was a "rescue mission." Fraudulent also was the 1989 Bush attack on and occupation of Panama. The bombing of Libya and overthrow of Gaddafi was similarly viewed as limited action not constituting war. Maybe bombs should be reclassified as friendly hugs. Martin Luther King denounced the United States as the "greatest purveyor of violence in the world." We still live up to that, but our scribes are there to rationalize and justify our actions.

re: Elisabeth Malkin, "Trial of Ex-Dictator of Guatemala May Have to Restart," May 22, 2013.

The supporters of genocide in Guatemala still have power—witness the Constitutional Court's overturning the conviction of former President and

General Efrain Rios Montt. When, in 1954, at the prompting of United Fruit, the United States overthrew the popularly elected progressive President Jacobo Arbenz, it initiated a horrendous reign of terror that murdered hundreds of thousands of Guatemalans. Montt's conviction of genocide and crimes against humanity was opposed by the rightist Guatemalan business federation (Cacil) and much of the military. Montt was a favorite of the Reagan administration, which also sponsored death squads in El Salvador and elsewhere. He illustrates the long record of US foreign policy supporting oligarchies, rather than the common people. Our unofficial sponsorship of death squads and genocide may have abated, but not our doting on the wealthy, both at home and abroad.

re: Mark Landler, "Obama Appoints Rice to Key Post on US Security," June 6, 2013.

Protecting human rights, freedom, and democracy has provided a splendid facade for US intervention, whether in Vietnam, Nicaragua (Reagan's thuggish "freedom fighters"), dismembering Yugoslavia, or intervening in Libya (where the more likely reasons were finance, oil, gas, and water). There are few things more nauseating than Susan Rice using Rwanda as her inspiration for fighting for human rights. She is a supporter, friend, and patron of Rwanda's President Paul Kagame whose invasion of Rwanda with Ugandan troops (and US complicity) slaughtered thousands—and thereby sparked the Rwandan government's genocide. Furthermore, Kagame, with his M23 terrorist mercenaries, is largely responsible for hundreds of thousands of Congolese deaths. Rice is fit neither to represent the United States nor to invoke human rights.

re: Thomas Kaplan, "Rivals Attack de Blasio on Past Support for Sandinistas," September 24, 2013.

Mayoralty candidate Bill de Blasio has been criticized by opponents for supporting the Nicaraguan Sandinistas. Unfortunately, the United States has a long and global history of supporting oligarchies while fighting those who cared for the lesser classes. In the 1980s, the United States flagrantly violated international law by mining Nicaraguan harbors and supporting the Contras, actions condemned in lopsided votes by the International Court of Justice in 1986. While the Sandinistas launched a massive literacy and health program, which the World Health Organization praised as a model, the Reagan administration supported an "army of racketeers, bandits, and murderers," as Speaker Tip O'Neill rightly described the Contras. Are opposition candidates Adolfo Carrion and Joseph Lhota suggesting we should support more bandits and murderers?

re: Elisabeth Malkin, "Guatemala's Highest Court Overturns Genocide Conviction of Former Dictator," May 21, 2013.

When, in 1954, at the prompting of United Fruit, the United States overthrew the popularly elected progressive President Jacobo Arbenz, it initiated a horrendous reign of terror that murdered hundreds of thousands of Guatemalans. Only one major actor, former President and General Efrain Rios Montt, was convicted of genocide, a conviction overturned by Guatemala's highest court at the bidding of the rightist Guatemalan business federation (Cacil). Mass murderer Montt was a favorite of the Reagan administration, which also sponsored death squads in El Salvador and elsewhere. He illustrates the long record of US foreign policy that favored existing oligarchies, rather than the common people. Our unofficial sponsorship of death squads and genocide may have abated, but not our continued support of the wealthy, both at home and abroad, at the expense of the less favored.

re: Michael R. Gordon, "A 'Good War' with Iraq in '91 Had Its Flaws," January 1, 2013.

Michael Gordon focuses on whether or not the (elder) Bush administration should have used its victory in the Gulf War of 1991 to topple Saddam Hussein.

He might have mentioned another important "flaw": whether the Bush administration tricked Hussein into invading Kuwait by having the US ambassador to Iraq, April Glaspie, assure Saddam that the United States had "no opinion" concerning Iraq's relations with Kuwait—which Hussein understood to be a green light for the Iraqi invasion of Kuwait that followed shortly after. As for a presumed boon resulting from the quick Gulf War victory—that it served to kick the "Vietnam syndrome" so that we could feel free again to attack other countries—that proved to be a boon or freedom we would have been better off not having.

Health

re: Robert Pear, "House GOP Again Votes to Repeal Health Care Law," February 4, 2015.

For the fifty-sixth time since 2011, the House Republicans have sought to dismantle the Affordable Care Act, which has given adequate health insurance for millions who did not have it. Has anyone ever heard of a major political party, at any time in history or anywhere, that for years has publicly declared its primary objective to be not general welfare, not jobs or the economy, not national security—but rather to prevent millions of their fellow citizens from getting adequate medical care? Tragically, the Republican Party has become the first major party in history to do just that. How can we fail to ask, incredulously, "Who are these people?"

re: Sabrina Tavernise, "Mortality Drop Seen to Follow '06 Health Law," May 6, 2014.

Since it adopted mandatory health coverage in 2006, Massachusetts's mortality rate fell about 3 percent in the four years afterward—as compared with mortality rates in other states. This translates nationally into seventeen thousand fewer deaths per year. Since Massachusetts's population is in many ways more favored than in other states, this suggests that the forty-five thousand annual deaths due to lack of medical insurance and coverage (estimated by a 2009 Harvard study) is pretty accurate. The data makes us wonder what kind of political party would declare its highest objective to be to repeal Obamacare—that is, to maintain this death toll by depriving fellow citizens of decent health care.

re: Editorial, "The War over Health Care Exchanges," July 27, 2013.

Saving American Lives: The Butt of Republican Fury

It's regretfully and shamefully true that the Republicans are trying everything to undermine or void Obamacare. In 2009, a Harvard study indicated that nearly forty-five thousand people prematurely died yearly from lack of health coverage and care. Obamacare would substantially slash that number, but this apparently infuriates Republicans. It's time to ask them pointedly: how many more American deaths would satisfy you—eighty thousand, two hundred thousand, eleven million? It's more than tragic to have such a powerful party rage at an attempt, however defective, to save American health and lives. Extending Medicare to all Americans would have been much better. But Obamacare is the only life vest in play today.

re: Janice Lynch Schuster, "Invitation to a Dialogue: Legalizing Aid in Dying," March 27, 2013.

What would a sadist recommend?

As Ms. Schuster notes, millions suffer a living death, which they have no right to deliberately shorten. The question of legalizing the right to die has stumped many who are not ideologically or theologically adamant in opposing it. But sometimes baffling issues can have a reliable guidepost. My rule of thumb is to ask, "What would a sadist want?" and then do the opposite. This also presupposes that we, and not the state, own our own bodies—a thought that would shock many "small government" advocates.

re: Ezekiel Emanuel, "Four Myths About Doctor-Assisted Suicide," October 28, 2012.

Ezekiel Emanuel seems to think that the poor don't suffer from "depression, hopelessness, and fear of loss of autonomy and control," the major reasons he finds for the wealthy to benefit from euthanasia or doctor-assisted suicide, which he opposes. Nor apparently, do the poor suffer from economic worries, a major problem for families of dying patients, which Emanuel doesn't even mention. Therefore, according to him, that suicide option doesn't interest or benefit the poor. Instead of legalizing this kind of suicide, he recommends better care for the dying and better conversations with physicians, something already provided for in those states permitting doctor-assisted suicide. It's hard to tell which is sillier, his diagnosis or his recommendation.

re: Manny Fernandez, "Perry Declares Texas's Rejection of Health Care Law 'Intrusions,'" July 10, 2012.

Governor Perry has become the only governor to reject in writing the building of the exchanges provided by the Affordable Care Act. The fact that 25 percent of Texas's population has no insurance, including over a million children, does not faze him. For all we know, he might even be proud of the fact this is the highest rate in the nation. In rejecting the billions of federal dollars that expanded Medicaid would have brought, he jeopardizes the well-being of Texans, some four thousand of whom die yearly from lack of medical coverage. Perry trumpets his Christianity—while conveniently overlooking or contradicting virtually every socially relevant passage of the New Testament. If Christianity means cruelty, he has a point. However, this certainly is not a compassionate conception of Christianity, especially from a self-advertised champion of pro-life stances.

re: Herszenhorn and Pear, "Health Care Overhaul Bill Passes Crucial Senate Test," November 22, 2009

Health Reform and the Republican Party of Death

After 176 of the 177 Republican House members did two weeks ago, thirty-nine of the forty Republican senators (Senator Voinovich was absent) opposed proceeding with health reform, thereby serving to perpetuate the yearly death toll of nearly forty-five thousand Americans, which a recent Harvard University study attributed to lack of health insurance and care. This does not include deaths due to inadequate health coverage.

This stamps the Republican Party as the Party of Death. Having long opposed a living wage, the Party of Death now desperately tries to scuttle health reform. "We cannot afford it, it's too costly," has been a major mantra for opposing such desperately needed reforms.

When it comes to killing and war, including needless wars, for the Party of Death there is always ample money. But when it comes to saving lives—why, the money just isn't there. With such an attitude, the Republican Party has truly earned itself the title of the Party of Death.

Ideology

**re: Dan Bilefsky, "Nazi Salute by Royals from 1930s Stirs Debate,"
July 21, 2015.**

It's too bad the controversy over the old film clip showing Princess Elizabeth (later Queen Elizabeth II), while three or four years old, making a Nazi salute, along with the queen mother and the future Edward VII, who did sympathize with Nazis. Many upper class Englishmen and Europeans did, which is the real point generally ignored by those who want superficial explanations of Nazism, as if it resulted merely from the magnetism of a maniacal Hitler. In fact, Nazis and Fascists, whether in Germany, Italy, Spain, or Portugal, enjoyed the financing and support of many members of the dominant classes who were thrilled at the crushing of labor unions and leftists—and therefore saw no reason to combat Hitler, or Franco's invasion of Spain. It's the factor of class interests that is nearly always ignored in these superficial discussions of Nazis and Fascists.

re: Paul Krugman, "The Laziness Dogma," July 13, 2015.

Paul Krugman is right that Republicans ignore economic realities and blame the poor and unemployed for their plight. A better economy, claimed Jeb Bush, would require that workers work harder and become more productive. Never mind, as Krugman points out, that American workers work more than workers in virtually every other wealthy country. He could have added that, as far as productivity is concerned, worker productivity since 1979 has doubled, while wages remained stagnant. Nearly all the increased wealth has gone to the top 1 percent, the ones likely to explain how unworthy the lesser classes are—and how meritorious they themselves are, even when they send the economy toppling.

re: George Packer, "Revolutionary Roads," review of Charles Murray, *Rebuilding Liberty without Permission*, and Chris Hedges, *Wages of Rebellion*, July 5, 2015.

It's typical for establishment voices to equate the extreme right and left, as if supporting health care, social security, living wages, etc., were the same as opposing them. Similarly, in complete disregard of the origins of the term "populist" in the 1890s, left and right (billionaire-backed) populists are also falsely equated. Besides being an example of this, George Packer thinks rightist Charles Murray, unlike leftist Chris Hedges, "has a case to make…supported by plenty of evidence." Naturally, he overlooks that mainstream Republicans and Libertarians (like Ayn Rand and Murray) share the same basic principle: screw workers, the weak and the poor, and worship the wealthy. As for alleged lack of evidence for leftists, just look at the huge transfer of wealth the last forty years from average Americans to billionaires. Big money has largely unlimited control over politics. Globally, in 2014, eighty super-rich persons held as much wealth as did half of humanity. That should make a pretty good case where Packer doesn't find one.

re: Nick Carasaniti, Richard Perez-Pena, and Lizette Alvarez, "Charleston Massacre Suspect Held as City Grieves," June 19, 2015. Frances Robles, Jason Horowitz, and Shaila Dewan, "Flying the Flags of White Power," June 19, 2015.

The gruesome killing of African Americans in their church, presumably by white supremacist Dylann Roof, naturally brings up again the issues of gun control and racism. But there's one issue nearly guaranteed not to be mentioned by the mass media: it is the utility of scapegoats—whether Jews, Blacks, Latinos, Asians, whatever—for dominant classes. When people in a society suffer from unemployment, poverty, threatened status, or forms of alienation, it would be dangerous if they turned in fury against those who rule society. Therefore, scapegoats are highly useful in deflecting that anger toward fellow sufferers. This factor cannot be mentioned by media run by the privileged, but I'll try.

re: Arthur C. Brooks, "The Thrill of Political Hating," June 8, 2015.

Mr. Arthur C. Brooks, president of the conservative American Enterprise Institute, well expresses the rightist tendency to cloud issues over. He criticizes political invectives without ever differentiating who gets well-deserved ones and who gets inappropriate ones. Conservatives like to play down power relations. They present society as a system of shared values and institutions, while omitting its class or power structure and exploitation. Mr. Brooks wouldn't bother to distinguish between those who would like to see millions of their fellow citizens deprived of health care, and those having compassion and a sense of justice. He wants equal good will to all, to the billionaires who would destroy our democracy, and to those who would preserve it. That's a stretch.

re: Eric Lichtblau and Alexandria Stevenson, "Hedge-Fund Magnate Emerges as a Generous Backer of Cruz," April 11, 2015.

The original and genuine populists arose in the 1890s, were honestly grassroots, defended labor unions and government intervention for justice, and were not funded by millionaires or billionaires. Today's populists (pseudopopulists would be more accurate) arose with billionaire Koch brothers' funding. Unlike the original populists, they back government deregulation. And they're funded by the big money the original populists opposed. The darling of Tea Partiers,

Senator Ted Cruz, it turns out, is similarly funded by big money; in particular, by rightist hedge-fund magnate Robert Mercer, whose network reportedly poured $31 million into the Cruz campaign. It's time the media began portraying Tea Party "grassroots populists" as what they are: pseudopopulist shock troops for the wealthy.

re: James Romm, "The Hands That Held the Daggers," review of Barry Strauss's *The Death of Caesar*, March 15, 2015.

Barry Strauss is right in seeing Caesar's murderers, led by Marcus Junius Brutus, to be primarily devoted to restoring the primacy of the Senate, which Caesar, as a populist champion, had undermined. The Senate stood for the rule of the wealthy. But too many historians have portrayed Brutus and his co-conspirators as foes of tyranny and champions of the republic. This includes Plutarch and that toady of the Senate, Cicero.

Caesar redistributed lands to his veterans and the poor, initiated a New Deal type of great building programs, and enacted severe laws against excessive interest rates—which must have infuriated Brutus, who was a usurer who lent money at 48 percent interest. The wealthy Senators had eliminated the reformist Gracchi brothers, who were champions of the lower classes. A century later, it was Caesar's turn.

re: Eric Lichtblau, "Surviving the Nazis, Only to Be Jailed by America," February 8, 2015.

Erich Lichtblau writes about how hundreds of thousands of Holocaust survivors spent months, if not years, imprisoned in decrepit camps while waiting for some country to accept them. A scathing report of their conditions was resented by General George Patton, who seemed to treat Nazi prisoners better than the Jewish victims, who he contended were "lower than animals." This was the fierce anticommunist Patton. The war against the Axis powers was also a war against a type of capitalism. But with the Cold War, it was largely assumed that anticommunism was a virtue, never mind that we had just defeated the greatest haters of communism, Hitler and Mussolini. A vicious type of anticommunism spread throughout the nation, culminating in the witch-hunts of McCarthyism. Any thug can be anticommunist. To be a democrat requires a different type of mentality.

re: David Brooks, "Building Better Secularists," February 3, 2015.

David Brooks criticizes the eighteenth-century Enlightenment philosophers for falsely believing we could be ruled by reason, whereas cognitive science shows that we are emotional, rather than rational, animals. Supposedly, these emotions can be put at the service of religious selfless agape—even though human beings, cognitive science would show, are creatures of self-love, rather than selfless. Furthermore, Brooks completely misunderstands the Enlightenment. Reason was not the basis, but the means, to a better society. Reason itself was propelled by emotions. Voltaire's criticism of church dogma and torture was visceral—but expressed with reason and satire. Rousseau made it perfectly clear that the basic emotions (self-love and compassion) were prior to reason. Reason was, or ought to be, the counselor, not the master of the emotions.

re: Sheryl Gay Stolberg, "A Vermont Senator Asks, Why Not a Socialist President," December 20, 2014.

Socialist Vermont Senator Bernie Sanders is considering running for president. One huge handicap, notes Ms. Stolberg, is "the socialist label." She's right, nothing could be more damaging. One reason for the problem is that all the corporate mass media have encouraged Americans to mock, ignore, misunderstand, or fear socialism. Socialism is often identified with the failed Soviet Union. One might as well assert that the demise of the Inquisition, absolute monarchies, slavery, and Nazi Germany—all in Christian nations—prove how rotten Jesus Christ and Christianity are. Both would be mistaken. Socialist Sanders supports universal single-payer health care, strong labor unions, and greater voter participation. Because he wants democracy, his pet peeve is the fearsome power of billionaires like the Koch brothers. Indeed, "Why not a socialist president."

re: Scott Shane, "Defending CIA, Cheney Revisits Bush-Era Debate," December 15, 2014.

Dick Cheney, before the attack on Iraq, falsely claimed that Saddam Hussein had weapons of mass destruction and supported Al Qaeda—and that American troops would be "greeted as liberators." Hard to top that, but the ex-VP managed when he defined torture, on NBC's Meet the Press, as what "terrorists did to three thousand Americans on 9/11." In other words, killing is torture, but he didn't mention that we were "torturing" throughout the Middle East. Nearly all Republicans agreed with Cheney in denouncing the Senate Intelligence Committee report that denounced torture. That's typical of the Rightist Brotherhood of Denial, and not just in the United States. The Japanese rightists, encouraged by the electoral victories of rightist Prime Minister Shinzo Abe, are denying Japanese war crimes. And let's not forget the rightist Europeans who deny the Holocaust. All these rightists seem to harbor an instinctive distaste for the truth. Considering what the facts are, that's understandable but not forgivable.

re: Editorial, "Hope and Anger at the Garner Protests," December 6, 2014.

The many instances of police abuse against minorities led you to cite the Justice Department's view that Cleveland's police department resembles more "an occupying military force than a legitimate law enforcement agency." This brings up the dual function of the police (and national guard, if necessary): (1) to protect citizens, and (2) to maintain the class structure of society. Concerning the latter, Adam Smith in *The Wealth of Nations* wrote: "Wherever there is great property there is great inequality. For one very rich man there must be at least five hundred poor, and the affluence of the few supposes the indigence of the many." To protect this class structure, he explained, was the major reason for the establishment of government. We have many billionaires and even more millionaires. This requires great poverty, which in turn requires the police to function as "an occupying military force."

re: Jason Weeden and Robert Kurzban, "Your Very Predictable Vote," November 4, 2014.

Jason Weeden and Robert Kurzban argue (not very originally) that people vote for their self-interest. It's not ideology or values that drive voters, but rather "the effect of policies on themselves, their families…" If that were true, the Republicans would only get 1 percent of the popular vote, the billionaires and multimillionaires who alone have substantially profited from the economic "recovery." To show that voters don't ignore their economic interests, the authors proudly point to the poorest fifth voting for only eight Republicans for every ten Democrats they support. If they really valued their economic interests, it would be zero Republicans for every eighteen Democrats. People are brainwashed by media (especially radio), and the propaganda millions poured by Koch-brother types, into scuttling their own welfare. The result of the elections today only confirms this.

re: Manny Fernandez, "Decision Allows Abortion Law, Forcing Thirteen Texas Clinics to Close," October 3, 2014.

The War on Democracy Requires the War on Women

A Republican-dominated three-judge panel of the Fifth Circuit Court of Appeals continued the rightist war on women by reducing abortion clinics in Texas to eight, from the original forty-one clinics Texas had last summer. That's when the rightist Texas legislature and governor began stripping women of abortion rights under the utterly phony rationale of protecting "the health and safety of Texas women." The war on women is not accidental. It's part of the war on democracy unleashed by the right and ably supported by the rightist Roberts Supreme Court, which allowed the political process to be flooded and dominated by big money. Rejection of women's rights and of democracy go hand in hand. Good examples are the structure of the Catholic church and several Muslim countries and fanatics.

re: Alan Cowell, "In Elections Across the World, Democracy Is a Matter of Definition," June 5, 2014.

Probably the most prostituted words politically are "liberty" and "democracy." As Alan Cowell mentions, elections have been invoked to demonstrate "democracy," even when occurring under dictatorial regimes boasting landslide victories, as in Egypt or Syria. It's quite true that it takes more than elections to have democracy. "Democracy" is not hard to define. It means literally "the rule of the people." That's "the rule of the people," and not the rule of money. In fact, the Ancient Greeks considered elections (as opposed to the lot) as undemocratic because of the opportunities they granted to the wealthy and well connected. So it's not only dictatorships, but also oligarchies or quasi-oligarchies like the United States who like to boast of their "democracy."

re: Andrew Higgins, "Populists' Rise in Europe Vote Shakes Leaders," May 27, 2014.

It's unfortunate how the media describes rightist parties as "populist," with the recent votes for the European Parliament providing the latest salient example. The original populists, who flourished in the United States in the 1890s, constituted a leftist movement, despite limitations of the time, including the racism of some populists. The populist party's platform of 1892 (the Omaha Platform) called for the direct election of senators, a graduated income tax, the abolition of national banks, and government ownership of railroads, telegraph, and telephone. It distrusted the "capitalists, corporations, national banks" that dominated both major parties, and strongly supported small farmers and workers. It believed that "the power of government—in other words, of the people—should be expanded...to the end that oppression, injustice, and poverty shall eventually cease in the land." In other words, virtually the exact opposite of the pseudopopulist Tea Party (in the United States) and European rightist parties.

re: Jennifer Steinhauer, "A Billionaire's 'Patriotic Giving,'" February 21, 2014.

Billionaire David M. Rubinstein should be rightly praised for his generous contributions, including to the Kennedy Center for the Performing Arts, the national zoo, and many other charities. While generosity is an undoubted good in itself, in this case, the flip side is alarming. As Rubinstein said, "The United States cannot afford to do the things it used to do." And therein lies the tragic flip side. The public (governments) can no longer attend to numerous public needs because of their iniquitous policies, including perverse tax structures. The governments (state and federal) previously provided for most public needs, but in the more recent decades they have suffered penury. This is largely due to policies that benefit big corporations and the 1 percent at public expense. Charity operates in inverse proportion to justice. The more unjust a society, the more the need for charity, such as Rubinstein's. When ancient Athens was a democracy, it provided for the public interest. But when it became an oligarchy during the Hellenistic period, it relied increasingly on the charity of the wealthy. This is one lesson of history we should seriously take to heart.

re: David Brooks, "The Opportunity Coalition," January 31, 2014.

David Brooks is no rabid Tea Party person. He urges compromise and "bipartisan groups"; he appeals to the American Whig tradition, which opposed the class divisions or warfare of the "populist Jacksonians." Brooks seems unaware of the fierce class warfare waged by the top 1 percent these last decades. In the 1950s, the top individual income tax bracket was 90 percent (still 70 percent in 1980), and now only 35 percent. Corporate taxes as a percentage of federal revenues dropped from 27.3 percent in 1955 to 8.9 percent in 2010—while individual income and payroll taxes increased from 58 percent to 81.5 percent. Virtually all recent income growth has gone to the 1 percent. The ratio of top CEO pay to average worker pay soared from 42:1 in 1960, to 100:1 in 1990, to over 300:1 in the 2000s. The 1 percent has waged an enormously successful class war that has dispossessed the lower and middle classes. Brooks doesn't see any of this as class war. Like the typical Republicans, he sees class war as occurring only when the victims seek to protect themselves.

re: Manny Fernandez, "'Texas Is Not America,' and Backs Its Senator in Defeat," October 19, 2013, and Gail Collins, "A Ted Cruz on Every Corner," October 19, 2013.

Cruz and the Tea Party: Our Fascists

Tea Party hero Ted Cruz is hailed for his "courage" in being willing to shut down the government in order to deny health care to millions of Americans. This "courage" of an egoistic bully evokes Nobel Laureate Sinclair Lewis's fictional account of fascism coming to the United States (*It Can't Happen Here*, 1935). The context is similar: economic crisis and insecurity. For both the Tea Party and Lewis's Fascists, there was the pseudopopulist posture attacking the banks and the powerful—while "big business just winked" and financed them (Lewis), as do today the Koch brothers et al. The fictional fascists were "minutemen"—with similar flag waving and phony appeal to tradition. Some also waved the Confederate flag. Both had many intolerant, hate-filled, cruel bullies who loved violence or guns. They both prized ignorance and dishonesty. Texas hero Cruz is an ominous omen hopefully restricted to Texas and only a handful of other deluded states.

re: Paul Krugman, "Insurance and Freedom," April 8, 2013.

Paul Krugman is right to question why the right's opposition to expanded health coverage, as well as its championship of the wealthy at the expense of the rest of us, is viewed as "a courageous defense of freedom." This is indeed the rightist conception of freedom, the right to dominate others and prevent the less fortunate from better conditions or equality. That classical icon of the conservative right, Edmund Burke, expressed it perfectly when he explained that among the "liberties" of the English people were aristocracy and monarchy—not democracy. Similarly, the South viewed Jim Crow laws as part of its "liberty." Since ancient Athens, democracy was viewed as requiring liberty through equality. But that's certainly not the view of our rightists today.

re: John Harwood, "Deep Philosophical Divide Underlies the Impasse," March 2, 2013.

The Responsibility of the Press: Don't Indulge Rightist Ideological Nomenclature

John Harwood sees the traditional philosophical battle to be between those who want to protect the vulnerable and those who want to limit government in order to "maximize liberty." Harwood unfortunately buys into the rightist conception of liberty: the right to dominate others. This conception of liberty was used to justify slavery and Jim Crow laws. It is invoked by the right in order to undermine the right to vote and allow money to dominate (as in *Citizens*

United). The right views itself as "pro-life" (though life ends at birth for most of them) and wanting to prevent "voter fraud"—a nice euphemism for flagrant voter suppression. The media should be more judicious in how it unthinkingly accepts the rightist branding of these basic issues.

re: Francois Furstenberg, "Invitation to a Dialogue: An American Paradox," September 26, 2012.

We Are All—and Not Just the Wealthy—Individuals

The obvious weakness of self-reliance or "rugged individualism" is that no individual by himself or herself builds cars, residences, schools, infrastructures, or even linen and clothing. There is an even greater weakness. The basic fact is that all human beings are individuals, not just the wealthy or successful ones. Therefore, to argue that government programs that benefit millions of individuals violate individualism means to oust the majority of people from being individuals, leaving only a privileged minority of "individuals" who believe government should act only for their own narrow interests.

re: Editorial, "New Frontiers of Extremism," August, 12, 2012.

The Republicans' Dirty Secret: They Don't Believe in Democracy

Representative Todd Akin (of "legitimate rape") may have irked the Republican leadership, but not because they don't share his views, but rather because he's exposed theirs. Most Republicans, including the leadership, do not believe a woman's body belongs to herself; it belongs to the state—which is closer to totalitarianism than to democracy. They would like to see unions destroyed, leaving big corporations to rule unchecked, which is incompatible with democracy. They believe that big (and secret) money should rule the political process. They even reject universal suffrage—an essential of democracy—by trying to strip millions of voters of their votes. In short, they don't really believe in the liberty and democracy they constantly invoke. That is their dirty secret.

re: Steven Erlanger, "What's a Socialist?" July 1, 2012.

I don't know if Steven Erlanger is ignorant or ideologically befuddled, but he seems to have no clue about the history and nature of socialism. He thinks the welfare state is what socialism means, which makes most of us "socialists." Incredibly, he has no awareness of the two essential principles of socialism: (1) that the major economic assets should be held by the community, not by a favored class, and (2) that there should be no class domination, if we are to be really free. Like so many people today who think democracy means the rule of wealth—or that liberty means concentrated wealth unfettered by governmental limitations—Erlanger has modified language to fit ignorance and rightist ideology. Indeed, many rightists indignantly agree with him that we're becoming, if we're not already, "socialists." I wonder what they would call real socialism.

re: Paul Krugman, "Wages, Wealth, and Politics," August 18, 2006.

The Old Republican Chestnut of Class Warfare

Paul Krugman rightly mentions that Democrats are fearful of championing social justice and equality lest they be "accused of practicing class warfare" and alienate their wealthy contributors. ("Wages, Wealth and Politics," August, 18, 2006) It's worth mentioning that this old Republican chestnut of class warfare conveniently overlooks how proficient our wealthy elites are in waging class warfare. Fighting against universal health care represents withering fire from the privileged classes—as do shifting tax burdens from the wealthy to the less fortunate, preventing living wages, degrading the environment for immediate profits, deregulating corporate power, and subjecting the legislative and electoral processes to the mandates of lobbyists and wealthy donors. All these are the heavy artillery of class warfare. It's not those who identify and resist such violence who initiate class wars. They simply recognize that they are the targets of upper-class economic bullets and have the gumption to say so.

Judiciary

re: Jeffrey Rosen, "John Roberts, the Umpire in Chief," June 28, 2015.

Chief Justice John Roberts likes to advertise himself as an impartial umpire who merely calls balls and strikes. Mr. Rosen strangely buys that advertisement, citing Roberts on marriage equality and the Affordable Care Act—though he does mention in passing Roberts's invalidating federal campaign finance laws and voting rights laws. Roberts may not be as strident as Justice Scalia, but for the most crucial question, who should rule society, he is as impartial as a frenzied fan. With no credible constitutional basis, he asserts that corporations are persons and money is speech. He suggests that minorities have no right to have their suffrage protected, and that eating away at women's abortion rights is quite kosher. His decisions are helping turn what's left of our democracy (where women rights are very strong) into oligarchy. This is an umpire who also bats and pitches.

re: Adam Liptak, "Angering Conservatives and Liberals, Chief Justice Defends Steady Restraint," June 27, 2015.

Good for the Supreme Court for upholding the Affordable Care Act and gay marriage rights! Good for Chief Justice Roberts for supporting the first, but not so good for his opposition to the latter. There, presenting himself as a champion of judicial restraint, he wrote, "In a democracy, the power to make the law rests with those chosen by the people." Chosen by "money" is more accurate, due to his decisions unleashing virtually unlimited political funding, which would turn democracy into oligarchy. He criticizes the majority for confusing their preferences with the Constitution: "the majority today neglects that restrained conception of the judicial role." Isn't that exactly what he did by viewing corporations as persons, overruling restraints on political spending, winking at the whittling down of abortion rights, and allowing the States to pummel universal suffrage? It's too bad he did not heed his own words on these most crucial decisions.

re: Adam Liptak, "Justices Decline to Hear Challenge to Wisconsin's Voter ID Law," March 24, 2015.

The rightist Roberts Supreme Court declined hearing a challenge to Republican Wisconsin's voter suppression law. The law required voters to present an ID on the flimsy and disproven grounds of a virtually nonexistent voter fraud. Some thought the rightist court's ruling to be a surprise, because it had temporarily halted the application of the law in 2014. But in context, it should have been no surprise, since it continues the Supreme Court's ongoing attempt to destroy democracy, first by allowing elections to be controlled by wealthy donors (*Citizens United v. FEC*, 2010; *McCutcheon v. Holder*, 2014); and secondly by encouraging voter suppression by its *Shelby County v. Holder* (2013) ruling, which gutted the 1965 Voting Rights Act. The Republican Party and the rightist Roberts Supreme Court are united in their determination to abolish democracy.

re: Erik Eckholm, "Oklahoma Carries Out First Execution Since Slipshod Injection in April," January 16, 2015.

The Oklahoma botched execution of Clayton Lockett, who writhed in agony for some forty minutes, amounted to torture. The Supreme Court refused to block the new cocktail of drugs used to execute Charles F. Warner (and Johnny

Kormondi in Florida) despite serious questions about its efficacy. In her sharp dissent, which was endorsed by three justices, Justice Sonia Sotomayor held that the three drugs risked causing unconstitutional severe suffering. But what else could you expect from the rightist Roberts Supreme Court when an eminent member of its conservative majority, Justice Antonin Scalia, actually declared recently that "nothing in the Constitution" prohibits torturing "suspected terrorists." One would think that Justice Scalia would be aware of the Eighth Amendment, which forbids "cruel and unusual punishments."

re: Nicholas Confessore, "Secret Money Fueling a Flood of Political Ads," October 11, 2014.

In *Citizens United v. FEC* (2010), which opened the floodgates of political financing, the rightist Roberts Supreme Court pretended to assume that this flood would be subject to disclosure. In fact, a reported 55 percent of broadcast advertising in the midterm elections stems from essentially secret donors. Nearly 80 percent of general election advertising supporting the Republicans came from secret money donated to groups like the Koch brothers' Freedom Partners. The rightist Roberts Supreme Court must be secretly thrilled.

re: Adam Liptak and Alan Binder, "Parts of Law Limiting Vote Are Restored by Justices," October 9, 2014.

The rightist Roberts Supreme Court keeps increasing its war on democracy and the universal suffrage it requires. Its key decision there was *Shelby County v. Holder* (2013), which emasculated the 1965 Voting Rights Bill. This led a number of Republican-controlled states to seek to suppress the voting of likely Democratic voters, especially minorities. The impartial Government Accountability Office indicated that new ID laws were likely responsible for lower turnout rates—especially among the young and African American voters—in 2012 in those states. Then less than two weeks ago, the rightist Supreme Court overruled a court of appeals decision that had struck down voting restrictions in Ohio. Yesterday, it did the same thing for North Carolina, overruling a Fourth Circuit Court of Appeals panel, although the latter had struck down only a few of the voter suppression provisions of that state. There is little question that if we had a democracy and a democratic Congress, the rightist Supreme Court justices would have been impeached.

re: Adam Liptak, "Supreme Court Delivers Tacit Win to Gay Marriage," October 7, 2014.

It may seem surprising that the rightist Roberts Supreme Court would allow gay marriages by refusing to review appeal courts' decisions that affirmed them. It's tempting to assume that the Roberts Supreme Court is following the evolution of public opinion, with nineteen states having already legalized such unions. But the Supreme Court is always ready to rebuff public opinion if it conflicts with its hidden agenda of transforming democracy into oligarchy—the major purpose of its decisions to open the floodgates of big money so it can control the political process. There are two better reasons for the court's attitude: Gay marriage doesn't threaten oligarchy the way women's rights do, which is why the court is harsh on the latter. Secondly, this gives the rightist court the chance to appear nonideological, in order to mask its highly ideological decisions. A very clever court!

re: Adam Liptak, "Supreme Court Blocks an Order to Restore a Unique Week of Early Voting in Ohio," September 30, 2014.

Democracy means the rule of the people, and not the rule of money. But in *Citizens United v. FEC* (2010) and *McCutcheon v. FEC* (2014), the rightist Roberts Supreme Court did its best to have big money dominate the political process. Democracy requires universal suffrage. The rightist Roberts court severely undermined that by emasculating the 1965 Voting Rights Act in *Shelby County v. Holder* (2013). To dot the *i*, the rightist Roberts court yesterday overruled the Sixth Circuit Court of Appeals, which had blocked Ohio from cutting the only week that permitted the same-day registration that minorities rely on (*Husted v. NAACP*, No. 14A336). In short, the rightist Roberts court is determined to destroy democracy. No one should be fooled by their hypocritical rationalizations (such as, corporations are persons) that are not even worth refuting.

re: Alan Blinder, "Conservatives See Potential in Tennessee Judicial Races," August 6, 2014.

Conservative and wealthy organizations, like the Koch-backed Americans for Prosperity, are trying to fill state judicial offices with right-wingers—not just in Tennessee but nationally. We can see from the Roberts Supreme Court how our democratic institutions are being dismantled by virtually unlimited (and often secret) donations by the wealthy. The right is seeking the same objectives for state judiciaries.

Before we shrug this off, it will be good to remember that, during the Weimar Republic, most judges had been appointed by the imperial government before World War I and disliked democracy. They sympathized with rightists paramilitary groups. The Kapp Putsch leaders (1920) were not punished. In the Munich Putsch of 1923, General Erich Ludendorff avoided prison, while Hitler received the minimum sentence allowable for high treason: five years, of which he actually served only eight or nine pampered months.

We had better beware of the impending "Koch-cratic" overthrow of democracy.

re: Jeff Shesol, "Rightward Bound," review of Laurence Tribe's and Joshua Matz's *Uncertain Justice*, and Bruce Allen Murphy's *Scalia*, *New York Times* Book Review, July 6, 2014.

Jeff Shesol is right to question the doubts expressed by Laurence Tribe and Joshua Matz on the ideological complexion of the Roberts Supreme Court. There is no question that it is a rightist court, one that is actually proceeding to destroy democracy. Democracy means the rule of the people, not the rule of money. But it's the latter that the court has enabled with *Citizens United v. FEC* (2010) and *McCutcheon v. FEC* (2014). Democracy requires universal suffrage, which the court undermined by gutting the Voting Rights Act of 1965 (*Shelby County v. Holder*, 2013). Where women are marginalized, democracy suffers. The Roberts court has nibbled away at abortion rights. In *Gonzales v. Carhart* (2007), it accepted partial birth abortion bans—"the first time," wrote the *New England Journal of Medicine*, the court prohibited physicians from using a needed medical procedure. In *McCullen v. Coakley* (2014), the court rejected the thirty-five-foot barrier enacted by Massachusetts to protect women from antiabortion harassment and violence—while claiming corporations have religion and don't have to pay for contraception (*Burwell v. Hobby Lobby*, 2014). It weakened unions (for example, *Knox v. SEIU*, 2012, and *Harris v. Quinn*, 2014) and, as James Liptak wrote (*New York Times*, May 5, 2013), was the most probusiness court in decades. So much for democracy and ideological doubts!

As for Scalia's "originalism," that's just fraudulent. How can you be an "originalist" and pretend corporations are persons (corporations were not even mentioned in the Constitution), or go along with executive wars (only Congress can declare war), or invent Second Amendment rights (*District of Columbia v. Heller*, 2008)

re: Editorial, "A New Battle for Equal Education," June 12, 2014.

Oh, How Innocent, Innocent the Right Is

The rightist Roberts Supreme Court polluted the political process by allowing virtually unlimited (even secret) contributions, thinking "innocently" they were merely protecting free speech. It scuttled the 1965 Voting Rights Act, "innocently" believing there were no more problems. The Republicans are trying to take the vote away from millions of voters (mostly minorities), "innocently" believing this would prevent (a virtually nonexistent) voter fraud. They stripped millions of women of abortion rights and protective health, "inno-cently" believing this would help women. Now comes California Judge Rolf M. Treu, undermining teacher tenure and unions, "innocently" trying to secure quality education for all—while "innocently" ignoring what really dooms these children: vast socio-economic inequalities. How do they get away with this? Because reputable, mainstream media—like this *New York Times* editorial—actually take them seriously.

re: Editorial, "The Court Follows the Money," April 3, 2014.

The editorial is right to point out that Chief Justice Roberts, while asserting "There is no right more basic in our democracy than the right to participate in electing our political leaders" (*McCutcheon v. FEC*), is really giving big mon-ey control of our society. The *McCutcheon* and other decisions by the Roberts court have undermined decades of congressional anticorruption efforts. Congressmen, the editorial points out, "unlike the justices, understand inti-mately how money in politics actually works." This implies the rightist justices are in good faith and naive, and don't understand the consequences of their actions. In fact, it is the opposite. It's precisely because their decisions give the wealthy control of our society and destroys democracy, that the rightist justices are acting the way they do. Their naiveté is as much a sham as their affection for the First Amendment.

re: Adam Liptak, "Justices, 5-4, Kill Key Spending Cap in Political Races," April 3, 2014.

The Roberts Supreme Court's War on Democracy

The Supreme Court's attempt to destroy democracy passed another mile-stone today with its *McCutcheon v. FEC* decision to strike down existing limits on how much an individual can spend on political candidates and committees. Until now, individuals were limited to $123,000 per election cycle; the court has raised this to millions. The rightist Roberts court had already struck down limits on political contributions in Arizona, Vermont, and Wisconsin—and allowed corporations to spend hundreds of millions with SuperPacs (*Citizens United*, 2010). The Roberts court has camouflaged its war on democracy by invoking "free speech" to mask its purpose. Since Ancient Athens, democracy has meant the rule of the people—not the rule of money. But it is precisely the rule of money that the rightist Roberts court is seeking to install. Similarly, the court has attacked that essence of democracy, universal suffrage, by scuttling the 1965 Voting Rights Act in *Shelby County v. Holder* (2013). This enabled Republican-controlled states to seek to disenfranchise millions of its citizens. Not surprisingly, the Republicans, who also seek to replace democracy with the rule of money, have hailed those judicial travesties.

re: Adam Liptak, "How Activist Is the Supreme Court?" October 13, 2013.

Adam Liptak shows that in terms of the number of laws overturned, the Roberts Supreme Court has been "less activist than any court in the last sixty years." This may be true, but it is meaningless, because a hundred trivial overturns is less significant than just one crucial overturn. Two of the Roberts court's overturns have indeed been crucial in undermining democracy: the *Citizens United* (2010) case and the recent *Shelby County v. Holder.* The first allowed big money to increase its control of elections, with the expenditures of federal and state elections surging to a record ten billion dollars in 2012 (John Nichols and Robert McChesney, *Dollarocracy*). The second case will permit stripping millions of citizens of the right to vote. Over thirty states have introduced legislation to curb voter access in the last two years, including ten states that require voters to show a photo ID. These two cases in themselves are more significant than most of the overturned legislation in the last sixty years.

re: Eknow N. Yankah, "The Truth about Trayvon," July 16, 2013.

The Roberts Court's Feigned Innocence and the Zimmerman Case

We should not overlook the impact of the Supreme Court winking at taking the vote away from black people (and Hispanics) in *Shelby County v. Holder*. It did this by pretending racism was no longer a serious fact imperiling voting rights by asserting smugly, "Our country has changed." No concern about the blatant attempt in Republican states to suppress the vote of minorities—or the fact that the wealth gap between blacks and whites had mushroomed from $85,000 in 1984 to $236,000 by 2009, or that blacks are unemployed at twice the rate (and imprisoned at 6 times the rate) of whites. Let's just all pretend there's no problem. Thus did the court give its imprimatur to racism, provided it be cloaked in feigned innocence. And that innocence permeated the entire Zimmerman trial.

re: Adam Liptak, "Justices Void Oversight of States Issue at Heart of Voting Rights Act," June 26, 2013.
Editorial, "An Assault on the Voting Rights Act," June 26, 2013.

The Right and the Roberts Court Don't Believe in Democracy

"Our country has changed," explained Chief Justice Roberts in justifying the effective nullification of the Voting Rights Act of 1965.

Indeed, it has. In 1976, the top 1 percent garnered 8.9 percent of the national income. By 2007, that had changed to 23.5 percent (back to 1928 levels). In 1980, the top CEOs earned forty-two times more than their workers. This had mushroomed to 354 times by 2012. Labor unions have been decimated, leaving corporate and financial power virtually unchecked. The *Citizens United* decision (2010) made sure these inequalities could be transferred to the political scene. The simple fact is that the right—Republicans, Tea Partyers, and the

Roberts Supreme Court—simply doesn't believe in democracy (the rule of the people). It believes in the rule of money, not people. Voter suppression, which the court in effect just upheld, shamefully confirms this.

re: Editorial, "The Anti-Union Roberts Court," June 23, 2012.

The Roberts court, in *Knox vs. SEIU*, takes offense at some union dues being used for political purposes without the explicit consent of nonmembers. It wants to substitute an unprecedented opt-out rule for the traditional opt-in rule. The antiunion bias of this decision clearly emerges from its failure to demand the equivalent from corporations. If the latter were forbidden to use corporate funds for political purposes without the explicit consent of its members or customers, that would be a good balance—but not one you can expect from the rightist Roberts court, which won't be satisfied until the Koch brothers have been crowned the co-kings of the United States.

MEDIA

re: Randal C. Archibold, "Ex-President of Haiti Put under House Arrest," September 13, 2014.

I can understand that Randal Archibold wants to echo the official line on foreign affairs. That is typical, though it cannot change what the facts are. American foreign policy is, virtually without exception, dedicated to supporting wealthy oligarchies throughout the world. It takes deep offense at those countries—like Venezuela, Chile, Nicaragua, Cuba, Dominican Republic, Grenada, etc.—that at some point favored the less-privileged classes. Haiti under Jean-Bertrand Aristide was such a country. Aristide cared for, was loved and elected by, Haiti's common people. This was unforgivable. He did not fall "out of favor" and was not corrupt. We did everything we could to undermine him, and finally kidnapped him in 2004 to Africa. He never "left the country" voluntarily. He remains popular enough that the president puppet we put in, Michel Martelly, had his judge place Aristide under house arrest. Haiti is one of many countries that require, but do not get, balanced reporting.

re: Peter Baker, "Chairman of Benghazi Board Defends Its Decision Not to Question Clinton," May 13, 2013.

How the Media Encourage Fraud

It's bad enough that the Republicans want to use the Benghazi issue (the 2012 Libyan Islamic attacks that killed several Americans, including Ambassador J. Christopher Stevens) to smear President Obama and, even more, potential 2016 Democratic presidential candidate Hillary Clinton. It's worse that they're given front-page coverage by the media. Even worse is the media ignoring outright fraud by some leading Republicans, such as the chair of the House Oversight and Government Reform Committee, Darrell Issa. On *Meet the Press* this Sunday, Chairman Issa complained, among other things, of the failure of the Obama administration to provide enough security for embassies abroad. Incredibly (!) David Gregory didn't even mention that Issa and the Republicans sought to cut $331 million for fiscal 2012 for that very embassy security. With media like that, no fraud need be timid.

re: Jennifer Steinhauer, "A Shadow Long Foreseen," December 31, 2012.

The Phony Rightist Equivalency

A major reason our political system hits so many impasses is the lack of an educated citizenry, resulted from distortions by mass media reporting. A major aspect of this distortion is the false equivalency given to forces that are not at all equivalent. It would be like according equivalency in physics to what an Einstein would think, compared to the views of the village idiot; or giving the same weight to the testimony of a murderer as to witnesses of the crime. Politically, this means giving equivalency to the Republican view of things—the party that has abused the filibuster and debt limit ceilings the most in our history, and that stands for whatever benefits billionaires at whatever cost to the public—with the Democrats many of whom have at least some sense of governing for all people, not just the wealthy. This false equivalency is exactly what distorts Jennifer Steinhauer's reporting of the present impasse on the "fiscal cliff." Both parties are supposedly equally to blame, both are equally intransigent, or both are equally distrustful. It's that kind of biased reporting that leads to an ignorant public, which leads to the current impasses so damaging to our country.

Oligarchy

re: Ashley Parker. "Trump Attacks as Republican Rivals Court Donors at Koch Retreat," August 8, 2015

Though better known for his outrageous statements, occasionally Donald Trump comes up with a valid one. And he did, concerning "all the Republican candidates that traveled to California to beg for money etc. from the Koch Brothers," referring to the Koch-led gathering of wealthy donors in Dana Point. Calling them "puppets," Trump mocked the "beg-a-thon," as the candidates, especially Scott Walker, vied in courting and soliciting the billionaires. This suggests these candidates are indeed puppets, eager to have their strings pulled by the Koch-type puppet masters. Perhaps Trump's remarks can help convince the two-thirds of Americans, who think the country is going in the wrong direction, that the problem lies essentially with the puppet masters, rather than with the puppets, themselves.

NOTE: according to a *New York Times* analysis, less than 400 families accounted for almost half of all the money raised in the campaigns so far (July 2015)

re: Editorial, "Big Business and Anti-Gay Laws," April 4, 2015

The Politics of Skins and Bones

Your editorial rightly points out that big corporations have financed politicians who combine rightist social views (e.g., anti LGBT, anti-women) with support of big business. It suggests this financial backing should stop. But Big Money knows what it's doing. It's the politics of skins and bones. It gets the meat, while the fundamentalists get the skins and bones – primarily, the opportunity to beat up on hapless women (the wealthy ones aren't affected) by depriving them of abortion, contraception, and disease protection rights. If the fundamentalists get out of hand, Big Money quickly slaps them down, as in Indiana and Arkansas [who initially passed anti LGTB legislation, before repealing them]. In the meantime, it can always count on their votes. Those are not about to go to the Democrats. It's the fundamentalists who should ask for some of the meat.

re: David Brooks, "The Temptation of Hillary," 3-6-15

The bugbear of Republicans/Rightists has long been equality, real equality. David Brooks is worried that Democrats, led by Hillary Clinton, are changing their focus from "human capital" to greater equality ("redistribution"). The right policies would, on the contrary, focus on "human capital" – essentially increasing workers' productivity through education. Brooks seems to ignore that a 143 per cent growth in workers' productivity (Economic Policy Institute) from 1973 to 2013 was accompanied by stagnant wages. He thinks skills lead to concentrated wealth, rather than a market economy, which reduced the number of unionized workers from nearly one-third, forty years ago, to 11.1 per cent today. During that time, the top 0.1 percent of families increased their percentage of household wealth from 7 per cent to 22 per cent. Top CEOs earned 20 times what typical workers earned in 1973; this has mushroomed to some 300 times more recently. During the same period, top individual and corporate tax rates plummeted. This is how power, not skills, works. This is how our oligarchy, not education, works.

re: Nicholas Confessore, "'16 Koch Budget Is $889 million," January 27, 2015

Times are changing to the Right. After being secretive for so long, the Koch brothers now brazenly parade the nearly $1 billion their network is ready to spend in 2016. What the real figure is, we'll never know. One thing the Koch brothers are doing is to justify Cuban authorities' reluctance to hold elections American-style. If unlimited amounts of funds are permitted to corrupt the system, as in this country, that is an excellent argument against holding these ironically-call "free" elections. For sure, the Cubans should have democracy, but a real one, not a sham one like here.

Republicans

re: Patrick Healy, "Walker, Viewed as 'Authentic,' Aims for 'Smart' in the '16 Race," July 13, 2015.

Admiring voters describe Wisconsin Governor Scott Walker as "authentic." He's authentic, all right—an authentic phony who lies through his teeth. In 2011, he claimed his campaign had discussed curtailing collective bargaining, which it did not. He claimed that "almost all" of the protestors at the capitol were from outside Wisconsin, which they were not. He pretended not to know whether President Obama was a Christian and loved this country. He "punted" on evolution when asked. He sounded the alarm about voter fraud when, according to Loyola professor Justin Levitt, only thirty-one credible cases of voter impersonation were found out in one billion ballots cast from 2000 to 2014. He's an advocate of "personhood" who will force women to undergo ultrasound before abortion—while trying to defund Planned Parenthood. He unsuccessfully tried to remove the words "search for truth" from the University of Wisconsin's mission. He has a point. Truth is the nemesis of this "authentic" man.

re: Maggie Haberman and Jonathan Martin, "Walker Turns to the Right in Iowa, and Sows Doubt Elsewhere," July 3, 2015.

It's hard to think how much further right the Koch brothers–backed Wisconsin Governor Scott Walker can go. He did shift rightward by calling for a constitutional amendment to undo the Supreme Court's endorsement of gay marriage, and he now stresses border security over immigration reform. But none of that is surprising from a Republican who worships the wealthy and abhors workers—to the extent that, when asked about how he would deal with terrorist ISIS, he answered, "If I can take on one hundred thousand protesters [union backers], I can do the same around the world." He later tried to backtrack, but his real feelings were out of the bag: American labor unions are the enemy, just like ISIS, and should be destroyed. And he's done his part by turning his once progressive state into a "right-to-work" (for less) state. They don't come more obnoxious.

re: Nikita Stewart and Richard Perez-Pena, "'I Will Never Be Able to Hold Her Again. But I Forgive You,'" June 20, 2015.

What a contrast between the forgiving compassion of the victims' families and the utter lack of compassion, even inhumanity, of Dylann Roof. His inhumanity had plenty of sources, especially in South Carolina, whose Confederate flag still glorifies slavery and present forms of racism. There are also the right-wing media that proliferate—including Fox News, not exactly a source of compassion. Aside from these cultural factors, there is the political factor. The dominant party in the South is a party utterly lacking in compassion, the Republican Party—a party that houses racists and hammers the weak and the poor by trying to decimate Medicaid and the safety net. It is the party that views it as a heinous sin to give millions of their fellow citizens adequate health care. It is also the party that would sacrifice the future of humanity for the sake of polluters' profits. It's certainly not from the Republicans that Dylann Roof would have learned compassion or humanity.

re: Editorial, "Republicans Take Aim at Poor Women," June 22, 2015.

The attempt by Republicans to defund Title X and Planned Parenthood would mean, as you wrote, having avoided 363,000 abortions (in 2012), which they call murder but don't seem to mind. They actually want to deprive poor women of cancer screening and STD testing. Nor did they mind that some forty-five thousand Americans died yearly until Obamacare (which they want to repeal) slashed that number. Furthermore, their pro-life record is pathetic, if you look at the basic causes of death: poverty, lack of health care, war, and environmental dangers. They also want to abolish sex education (in favor of failed abstinence programs), but it's not just sex education they fear, it's any education that would alert Americans to what Republicans really stand for. They can call themselves "pro-life" all they want, but their record is one of pro-death.

re: Steven Eder and Michael Barbaro, "Rubio Career Bedeviled by Financial Struggles," June 10, 2015.

Senator Marco Rubio's finances have been dogged by huge debts (over $1 million at times), financial irresponsibility, and intermingling GOP party funds with his private ones. This is hard to reconcile with his repeated championship of governmental financial austerity. Nevertheless, Mr. Rubio and his allies have tried to portray him as a self-made man who did not rely on wealthy friends or family and, like so many Americans, has struggled with debts. They have a point. Most indebted Americans have three houses, like Mr. Rubio. They typically have speedboats and luxury cars. Like him, most made three hundred thousand dollars as a lawyer—and received eight hundred thousand dollars from a publisher. Is there any indebted American who does not have a billionaire sponsor, like Mr. Rubio has? Yes, indeed, it's awfully hard for those of us hard-pressed for money not to identify with Senator Rubio.

re: Editorial, "Let the People Vote," June 5, 2015.

Nearly one-third of all eligible voters—over fifty million Americans— are not registered to vote. Far from seeking to remedy this dismal reality, Republicans are trying to add millions more to those deprived of the vote. They're doing this by various devices ranging from restrictive voter ID laws to cutting down early voting periods. The rightist Roberts Supreme Court has abetted this effort. This opposition to universal suffrage—an essential part of democracy—is accompanied by Republicans' opposition to the very meaning of democracy, the rule of the people. Instead, they labor too successfully for the rule of money. You mention a test of "what it means to be a democracy." The Republicans have flunked the test very badly, and we can only ignore this at our own peril.

re: Patrick Healy and Monica Davey, "Conservatives and Their Cash Lined Up Early Behind Walker," June 8, 2015.

Governor Scott Walker won the support of wealthy corporations like the Bradley Foundation and the Koch-backed Americans for Prosperity. He is "revered as a leader brave enough to face down unions and their liberal supporters." Indeed, he broke collective bargaining for public employee unions. But it's the valor of a bully. Unions are weak and getting weaker. Their combined assets would be just a fraction of either David or Charles Koch's assets of $41.5 billion each. Twenty-five states, including recently Wisconsin, have enacted antiunion "right-to-work" laws. Rightist donors flooded his campaigns with money that dwarfed what unions could contribute. He presented himself as striving for "change," by which he meant the same grinding down of the weak that rightists applaud. No wonder they love bullies like Walker.

re: Editorial, "Scott Walker's Effort to Weaken College Tenure," June, 6, 2015.

There's a limit on how much fraudulence one should tolerate from politicians. Scott Walker has crossed this limit. In 2011, he claimed his campaign had discussed curtailing collective bargaining, which it did not. He claimed that "almost all" of the protestors at the capitol were from outside the state, which was not true. This year, he pretended not to know whether President Obama was a Christian or whether he loved this country. His signing of a voter suppression law (photo ID requirements) was supposedly intended to prevent voter fraud, which hardly exists: one study showed that from 2000–2014, there were a mere thirty-one cases of voter impersonation out of a billion ballots cast. Now he wants to place university professors' tenure and other rights under the Board of Regents, which he mostly appoints. He earlier tried to remove from the university's mission the words "search for truth." He had a point. Truth is his nemesis.

re: Jeremy W. Peters, "Clinton vs. Rubio, Head to Head, Is a Scary Thought for Democrats," May 23, 2015.

Rubio's Yesterdays Reject Rubio's Tomorrows

An election pitting Senator Rubio against Hillary Clinton shouldn't be scary for Democrats. Even his Latin background is a mixed bag with his retreat on immigration, as former Governor Bill Richardson pointed out. Also, pampered Cubans aren't exactly beloved by other Latinos. In announcing his candidacy for president, Senator Rubio stressed breaking with the past: "Yesterday is over, and we are never going back." His problem is that his policies are all Republican yesterdays: opposing raising minimum wages; getting rid of capital gains, dividends, and estate taxes; being antichoice on abortion and pro-gun; undermining Medicaid and, like Paul Ryan, envisaging privatizing Medicare; being a hawk on foreign policy and wanting to keep the same failed policies on Cuba. There's nothing more old hat than presenting yourself as a figure of change. Who hasn't. If you want yesterday, vote Rubio. Nothing substantial to fear here.

re: Nicola Clark, "Low US Rail Spending Hurts Safety, Experts Say," May 21, 2015.

Nicola Clark reports that the United States comparatively spends much less on rail networks, and has a much worse fatality record, than European Union countries, Japan, and Australia. Japan's bullet train has never experienced derailment or fatalities in 51 years of operation. This is also true for decades of France's high-speed TGVs. That's because these countries are willing to spend what it takes, both for efficiency and human life. In Peter Davis's Vietnam documentary *Hearts and Minds*, we hear General Westmoreland fatuously declare, "Life is cheap in the Orient." This would seem to be truer of Republicans, who skimp on money for life—including railway safety or health insurance or infrastructure—but always find plenty of dollars for the military and killing.

re: Jeremy W. Peters, "GOP Hopefuls Now Aiming to Woo 47 Percent," May 4, 2015.

Leading Republicans like Jeb Bush, Scott Walker, and Senators Rubio and Cruz are pretending to care about the 47 percent spurned by Mitt Romney. They (not Bush) stress their humble beginnings and families—and one-dollar sweaters (Walker), but judging from their actions, here's what they really think. Jeb Bush: the way out of poverty is our traditional principles, which idolize the wealthy. Cruz: let's help the poor, providing we don't change the policies that impoverished them. Rubio: get rid of capital gains and estate taxes; social mobility is the thing—from millionaire to billionaire. Scott Walker: good old Ronnie Reagan, he certainly knew how to screw the poor, but I'm even better—I'll destroy unions (workers and the middle classes) and prevent raising the minimum wage—I got mine, so the hell with the rest of you. Hilarious—if they didn't have power.

re: Jonathan Weisman, "Congress Clears Path to Fast Deal on Pacific Trade," April 17, 2015.

If anything is clear in the muddled politics of Washington, it is that the Republicans deeply dislike, or even hate, President Obama. Their primary objective seems to be to block every initiative or program he favors, like negotiating peace with Iran. Therefore, one could have confidently expected the Republicans to oppose the Trans-Pacific Partnership (TPP) and the president's request to fast-track it. Most Democrats—and virtually every labor union— oppose it, while most Republicans—and major business groups—support it. What could have overcome this deep dislike of President Obama? In a word, religion. The Republicans devoutly believe in the Trinity: the dollar, money, and the holy gold. This overrides everything, as seen in yesterday's House vote to abolish the estate tax on millionaires. One can count on their piety.

re: Editorial, "A Shortage of Funds for Food Safety," April 9, 2015.

According to estimates from the Center for Disease Control and Prevention, every year some one in six Americans get sick, and three thousand die, from food-connected illnesses. The FDA obviously needs increased funding to protect our food supply. Yet Republicans appropriated less than one-half the amount needed, according to estimates from the Congressional Budget Office. How could we expect the Republicans to care, when they're furious that President Obama tried to cut down the number of Americans dying from lack of medical care—some forty-five thousand yearly (until the detested Obamacare kicked in to reduce substantially those numbers). It's a tragedy that so much of our government is controlled by the heartless and shameless.

re: Patrick Healy, "How Is Scott Walker Like Reagan? He'll Tell You," April 7, 2015.

Like virtually all major Republicans, Scott Walker reveres Ronald Reagan. And they're right on track. Reagan was heartless toward the poor, denying there was hunger and homelessness at the same time these were growing (if there was, it was their fault). Black leaders called him the most insensitive racially and morally in decades (he initially opposed making Martin Luther King's birthday a national holiday). He adored the rich, cutting their highest tax rates from 70 percent to 28 percent—as well as capital gains taxes. He was a bully abroad, ruthlessly invading hapless Grenada in 1983—while supporting dictators and death squads in Central America. He also loved the military, boosting their revenues so heavily that he nearly tripled the national debt. The essence of Reagan was captured in 1974, while governor of California. He denounced huge crowds of poor people seeking free food the Hearst family was forced to distribute by the SLA, who had kidnapped Patty Hearst: "It's just too bad we can't have an epidemic of botulism." That's the spirit today's Republicans revere.

re: Paul Krugman, "Imaginary Health Care Horrors," March 30, 2015.

Paul Krugman once again unmasks the major lies of Republicans concerning Obamacare. The Republican chair of the House Rules Committee actually claimed that the plan's extended coverage would cost every recipient $5 million, rather than the actual four thousand dollars per newly insured American. Republicans have also insisted that Obamacare is a "job killer," although private-sector jobs have grown substantially since its implementation. Of course, they don't talk about some sixteen million Americans happily benefiting from the law, which incidentally costs tax payers 20 percent less than initially estimated by the Congressional Budget Office. The unceasing stream of Republican lies, on this and other issues, have led Krugman to deplore this new era of "post-truth politics."

re: Jonathan Weisman, "Republican Budgets in Both House and the Senate Add to Military Spending," March 20, 2015.

Rightists generally are more willing than leftists to engage in war. The Taliban and ISIS are good examples—as are the Iranian and Israeli hard-liners who oppose important peace moves. In the United States, we have our own rightists who reject a nuclear control pact with Iran, and who imply we should attack Iran—with some even directly demanding such attacks, as did Texas Representative Louie Gohmert who declared, "It's time to bomb Iran." The military hawks have prevailed in both House and Senate by trying to circumvent the spending caps enacted by the 2011 Budget Control Act. Billions were added to the Pentagon through the gimmick of a "war account" not subject to that act. Increased military expenditures are matched by decreased civilian expenditures, as envisaged by Republican House and Senate budgets. A bad combination.

re: Paul Krugman, "Trillion-Dollar Fraudsters," March 20, 2015.

Paul Krugman is right that the proposed House and Senate Republican budgets exhibit a manipulative dishonesty perhaps unmatched in American politics. The savage cuts they propose in food stamps and Medicaid—and most likely in social security and/or Medicare—are rationalized by disproven trickle-down or supply-side economics. Their real purpose is to effectuate, as Krugman writes, "a huge transfer of income from the poor and the working class…to the rich." There is another purpose Krugman omits: to destroy democracy by substituting the rule of money for the rule of the people. This flows ineluctably from the transfer of wealth and income from the middle and lower classes to the wealthiest, who can thereby increasingly buy elections and the elected.

re: Michael Barbaro and Michael D. Shear, "Criticism Aside, Obama Has Stated Love for United States," February 23, 2015 and/or Charles M. Blow, "Who Loves America?" February 23, 2015.

Rudy Giuliani lied about President Obama not loving America—and in denying President Obama had ever expressed affection for America. In fact, if anyone does not love America, it's the Republicans. They rage against President Obama's attempt to cut down the forty-five thousand to fifty thousand who died yearly from lack of medical care. They dislike the 13 percent black and the 17 percent Hispanic minorities, whose votes they're trying to take away. They don't like workers, whose unions and wages they seek to torpedo. They dislike half the population—women—enough to try to strip them of abortion and contraception rights. They used to like the middle classes but prefer an economy that crushes them. They announced that President Obama's "priorities are going nowhere," which include the economic recovery of the country. One wonders how they can even like themselves.

re: Michael Shear and Julie Davis, "Obama Declares It's Time to 'Write Our Own Future,'" January 21, 2015.

Part of President Obama's middle-class focus, during his State of the Union address, dealt with his proposal of making our iniquitous tax system somewhat fairer. This would require tax cuts for the middle classes to be paid for by increasing the taxes of the ultra-rich. This modest proposal evoked the usual Republican charge of class warfare against the rich. What Republicans don't mention is that the wealthy have been waging a very successful class war against the middle and lower classes. The top individual income tax brackets were over 90 percent in the 1950s, down to less than 40 percent today. There were only some 450,000 millionaires in 1978 (and one billionaire). In 2013, there were 9,630,000 millionaires and 490 billionaires. In 1979 the top 0.1 percent owned 7 percent of the national wealth; in 2012 it was 22 percent. Who paid for these differences? The victims of the war—the lower and middle classes. Republicans don't view the war on expanded health care as class war. That's because they're not the intended victims.

re: Jonathan Martin, "In GOP, a Divide of Ideology and Age," January 8, 2015.

Much too much has been made of Republican divisions—between Tea Party types and establishment types, between younger and older Republicans, between more compassionate and less compassionate. Concerning the latter, Republican/Bush compassion is essentially crocodile tears compassion. Yes, there are differences in style, but when it comes to basic issues, the Republicans are and have been united on three fundamental principles: (1) crucify the weak and the poor (for example, cutting down on food stamps, unemployment insurance, and social security), (2) decimate the middle classes (through free markets, outsourcing, and destroying labor unions), and (3) worship the Golden Calf and the wealthy (virtually all Republican policies). Even the antiabortion GOP policies are directed only against poor women; wealthy ones can always manage, at home or abroad.

re: Jonathan Weisman, "Many in GOP Offer Theory Default Wouldn't Be That Bad," October 9, 2013.

The Republican Party of Ignorance

Just when America's two greatest creditors, Japan and China, are sounding the alarm over the perils of a default, an increasing number of Congressional Republicans are making light of the possible consequences. Unfortunately, this is not surprising from the Party of Ignorance. A 2012 Dartmouth poll showed that by almost a 3 to 1 ratio, Republicans still believed President Obama was born in another country. A 2011 Gallup poll found that 46 percent of Americans denied evolution and believed God created human beings in the last ten thousand years or so. The creationists are about the most Republican group in the country. In 2012, the American Sociological Review concluded that trust in science among conservatives and frequent churchgoers had hugely declined since 1974. With a constituency like that, Republican leaders can feel safe to voice any stupidity that comes to their minds.

re: Jonathan Weisman and Jeremy W. Peters, "House Leaves US on Brink of Shutdown," September 29, 2013.

Dear Mr. President,

Speaker John Boehner and Majority Leader Eric Cantor have urged you to negotiate and compromise. We are willing to compromise, while of course honoring our principles. This is what we suggest:

(1) Concerning food stamps and the poor, while we would like to cut off all the limbs of the poor and unemployed, we could be

open to just chopping off their legs, while leaving their arms intact.

(2) Concerning oil and gas interests, while we would prefer giving all of western United States to the oil companies, we're willing to just let them own California.

(3) Concerning the Affordable Care Act, some forty-five thousand Americans die yearly from lack of medical coverage and care. We think that's a much too low number, and on this one, we're not willing to compromise one whit.

We hope we have shown you how to compromise while remaining principled.

Yours truly,

The House Republicans

re: Nicholas D. Kristoff, "Suffocating Echo Chamber," September 26, 2013.

Nicholas Kristoff is not the first to compare Senator Ted Cruz to Don Quixote. It would be good if he were the last, because the comparison is completely misleading.

Don Quixote is not a manipulator, like Cruz. He does not use propaganda to win support. He sees knighthood as being at the service of the weak, injured, and oppressed, whereas typical Republicans, including Cruz, believe (however they disguise that belief) that only the wealthy and powerful really matter. Don Quixote may be delusional, but he acts in good faith. It's highly implausible to see Don Quixote raging against saving people's lives by giving them health insurance. There is nothing sneering, condescending, or dishonest about Don Quixote. He would make a very poor Joe McCarthy, whereas Cruz would fit right in. The comparison does a real disservice toward understanding either Cruz or Don Quixote.

re: Manny Fernandez, "Texans Rebut Governor on Expansion of Medicaid," March 5, 2013.

With 24 percent of the population not covered, Texas has the highest rate of uninsured residents in the country. Nevertheless, Governor Rick Perry has refused to expand Medicaid for Texans under the Obamacare provisions, which would extend coverage to over one million less fortunate Texans. However, can anyone think of anything of less interest to Governor Perry than the well-being of his poorer citizens? No doubt, that's because he's such an avowed "Christian."

re: Michael D. Shear and Jonathan Weisman, "Romney Strategists Say They'll Stay the Course Amid Focus on Abortion," August 23, 2012.

Akin as the Perfect Mirror of the Republican Party

Mitt Romney's campaign hopes to dissociate itself from Representative Todd Akin (the "legitimate rape can't lead to pregnancy" guy). "Please show me the candidate in this country who says he agrees with Todd Akin," said a GOP spokesman. A much greater challenge would be: "Please find a Republican who does NOT agree with Akin on the major issues." Akin joins Representative Paul Ryan in wanting to abolish abortion even in cases of rape and incest— and in wanting to defund Planned Parenthood. Like Ryan, he would privatize Medicare. He voted against stimulus bills for the economy; he favors a constitutional amendment banning same-sex marriages; he votes against alternative energy and for the oil and gas lobbies. He is rated 90 percent by the Chamber of Commerce and has a strong antiunion record. In short he is a perfect mirror image of the Republicans—and that is exactly what frightens them so much, that the public will discover this.

Bush's "Politics of Skins and Bones"—2006

It's not surprising that David Kuo felt that President Bush's top advisers, while happy to use them, had contempt for his evangelical supporters ("Book Says Bush Aides Dismissed Christian Allies," October 13, 2006). This corroborates the long-term "Politics of Skins and Bones" of the GOP, whereby those really respected—the wealthy (both personal and corporate) are given the "meat" of tax favors, deregulation, union-busting, shredding the environment, and ruthless globalization. As for the small-fry Republican voters, evangelical or not, they just get "skins and bones," that is, such wedge issues as abortion, gays, school prayers, and flag-waving. No "meat" for them: no job security, no living wages, no adequate schools, and no health coverage. The "meat" only goes to those who are respected. Apparently, this does not apply to the evangelicals.

Highest Bush and Cheney Priority: Torture?—2006

President Bush and Vice President Cheney traveled to Congress to influence passage of legislative authority to bypass the Geneva Conventions and use "alternative interrogation practices" (their euphemism for torture) on suspected terrorists ("Rebuff for Bush on Terror Trials in a Senate Test," September 15, 2006). Have Bush and Cheney ever gone together to Congress to seek job preservation for workers, environmental protection, infrastructure maintenance, improved schools, or better health coverage for Americans? No, these crucial issues pale in importance compared to the right to torture—allegedly and most dubiously required for national security.

What a monstrous testament on the priority of values for this power-obsessed administration!

re: The Myth of Saint Reagan, Op-Ed sent 4-18-2015.

It's hard to find a leading Republican who does not praise or identify with President Ronald Reagan. They have chosen their patron saint well.

Reagan was heartless toward the poor, denying that hunger and homelessness were problems at the very same time these were painfully growing—and if there was a problem, it was their fault. Under Reagan, wrote former House Speaker Tip O'Neill, a "hatred of the poor...developed all across America." Similarly today, Mitt Romney can bewail the 47 percent of Americans who feel "entitled to health care, to food, to housing, to you-name-it." His 2012 running mate, Paul Ryan, had identified 30 percent of Americans as "takers." In Reagan's spirit, Republicans seek to cut safety nets, including food stamps and Medicaid, while also seeking to take away voting rights. Reagan loved to tell the story of a black welfare woman living lavishly in Chicago by collecting some 103 welfare checks under different names. He was told repeatedly the story was false, but he continued using the anecdote, showing the same contempt for facts and truth characterizing today's Republicans.

Conversely, coached by his wealthy rightist businessmen "kitchen cabinet," Reagan, like today's Republicans, adored the wealthy, whose top tax brackets he cut from 70 percent, when he took office, to 28 percent. He rationalized this by "supply-side economics," a euphemism for trickle-down economics, as Reagan's budget director, David Stockman, acknowledged. Stockman also admitted that "supply-side [trickle-down] economics" was just a Trojan horse to bring down top tax rates.

Black leaders viewed Reagan as highly insensitive racially and morally. He initially opposed making Martin Luther King's birthday a national holiday—and was viewed by the South African apartheid regime as their greatest supporter, internationally. It's in the Republican Party today that racists find their most congenial home.

In the early 1960s, Reagan denounced a Medicare proposal. He called the bill "socialist." It would destroy democracy: "You and I are going to spend our sunset years telling our children...what it once was like in America when men were free." Medicare's huge success has reduced today's Republicans to seek privatizing it through vouchers.

In foreign affairs, like today's neocons, or Republican hawks like Senators John McCain and Lindsey Graham, Reagan loved the military and aggression. He boosted military expenditures to such an extent that he nearly tripled the national debt. He ruthlessly invaded tiny, hapless Grenada in 1983 because he didn't like its regime. The invasion was overwhelmingly condemned by the UN General Assembly, which deplored this "flagrant violation of international law" by 108 to 9 (mostly small dependent Caribbean islands), with 27 abstentions (including Reagan's staunchest ally, Margaret Thatcher's Great Britain). Reagan's reaction was a contemptuous "It didn't upset my breakfast at all," a radical contrast with the Declaration of Independence's appeal to "a decent respect to the opinions of mankind."

Similarly, Reagan tried illegally to arm the Nicaraguan "contras," whom he called "freedom fighters." "Murderers" and "bandits" would have been more accurate. He mined Nicaraguan ports—which was condemned by the UN International Court of Justice. The UN had praised Nicaragua for its health program. At the same time, Reagan supported and financed murderous "death squad" dictatorships in Central America.

The essence of Reagan was captured in 1974, while he was governor of California. He denounced large crowds of poor people seeking the free food that the Hearst family was forced to distribute by the SLA, who had kidnapped Patty Hearst. "It's just too bad we can't have an epidemic of botulism," he said. That's the spirit of today's Republicans.

Why Republicans Necessarily Must Deceive—Op-Ed, January 31, 2015. Updated: February 4, 2015. (Printed by *Santa Fe New Mexican* after rejection by *New York Times*.)

Rightist luminary Glenn Beck assured us that President Barack Obama is a "communist revolutionary" who hates white people. Highly prominent rightist commentator Rush Limbaugh stated "without equivocation that this man [President Obama] hates this country." Normally, giving health care to millions deprived of it would be a virtue. During the 2014 midterm elections, it was turned by Republicans into a heinous sin.

A study released in March 2012 by the *American Sociological Review* noted that faith in scientists and science was declining rapidly among conservatives and frequent churchgoers. In June 2012, a Gallup poll showed that 46 percent of respondents (most in highly Republican groups) rejected evolution. Almost one-third of Louisiana Republicans blamed President Obama for inadequate response to Hurricane Katrina—though Obama had not yet been elected president. It's not surprising that two moderate scholars, Thomas Mann and Norman Ornstein, concluded in April 2012 that the GOP is "unmoved by conventional understanding of facts, evidence, and science."

Now, it's tempting to dismiss rightist distortions and lies as simple political tactics, and there's some truth to that. Yet liberals and progressives, having an equal interest in winning elections, do not need to resort to such dishonesty. The contrast resides in that rightist/Republican values are fundamentally opposed to democratic ones, but there's no way that the rightists/Republicans can acknowledge this publicly in a society formally committed to democratic values. More specifically, democracy champions liberty as requiring equality, whereas the rightists/Republicans champion "liberty" in the opposite sense of safeguarding and even increasing existing inequalities. As Karl Mannheim pointed out in his classic *Ideology and Utopia*, inequality—economic, social, and political—has traditionally been and remains central to the rightist (ideological) perspective. This places the right on a collision course with democracy.

Democracy's conjunction of equality with liberty arose in the very origins of democracy in Ancient Athens. Aristotle noted the consensus (among both supporter and opponents) that democracy means "freedom based upon equality." The ideological right, however, has traditionally rejected equality, even claiming it threatened liberty. The French Revolution—still a favorite punching bag for rightists—affirmed the leftist principles of "liberty, equality, fraternity," which challenged and overthrew the aristocratic inequalities of the Ancien Régime. Vehemently opposed to that revolution was Edmund Burke, the hero of modern conservatives. Burke identified "our liberties" with maintaining the sharp class differences of his time, including an "inheritable peerage" and an "inheritable crown."

Today's rightists continue to oppose equality but cannot admit publicly that their concept of "liberty"—giving unfettered power to corporate, financial, and wealthy elites—is antidemocratic. Indeed, as if they were themselves champions of equality, they posture as "outsiders" or "populists" who attack the "elitism" of academics and liberals. Yet today's rightists seek to strip the vote from millions of Americans—under the specious rationale of preventing (a virtually nonexistent) voter fraud.

Consequently, the distortions of the right are in the very structure of rightist thought. As long as our society professes democratic values, the right is doomed to pretend to be what it is not. It does not matter whether these postures are truly believed or not. The conflict between the equality-based liberty of democracy and the right's commitment to ever-greater inequalities is inevitable. There is no way rightists can be honest—whether to themselves and/or to others—as long as they profess democratic values, while at the same time pursuing fiercely antidemocratic policies.

Voter Suppression

re: Amy Chozick, "Clinton Says GOP Rivals Try to Stop Young and Minority Voters," June 5, 2015.

[this was used for "Democrats" also]

Hillary Clinton singled out Governors Rick Perry, Chris Christie, and Scott Walker for their efforts to disenfranchise voters, especially the young and minorities. She mocked their rationale of "a phantom epidemic of election fraud." Indeed, Loyola University professor Justin Levitt, an expert on elections, showed there were only thirty-one credible incidents of voter impersonation out of one billion ballots cast from 2000 to 2014. Clinton criticized the Republican Supreme Court for gutting the 1965 Voting Rights Act, thereby permitting much more voter suppression. Since universal suffrage is essential to democracy, she asked, "What part of democracy are they afraid of?" Unfortunately, the answer is, "the whole of democracy itself." This is why the Republicans are turning the rule of the people into the rule of the wealthy, to accompany voter suppression.

re: Steven Yaccino and Lizette Alvarez, "GOP Is Enacting New Ballot Curbs in Pivotal States," March 30, 2014.

The Democrats are partly to blame for the Republicans' attempts to deny the vote to millions of citizens. In nine states since 2013 only, restrictions such as voter IDs, closing weekend voting, requiring birth certificates, and/or reducing early voting time, have been enacted by Republicans. While resisting these efforts, Democrats have amazingly not focused on the basic issue: universal suffrage as a requirement of democracy. And that is indeed—despite all their lies, obfuscations, and pretended concern for virtually nonexistent problems like voter fraud—what the Republicans are doing, rejecting democracy by rejecting universal suffrage. And that is exactly what the inept Democrats failed to but should have focused on—insisting that Republican candidates explain to their constituents why they reject democracy. But when it comes to fundamentals, the Democrats prefer, "see no evil, hear no evil, speak no evil," which is why "evil" has such an easy time clobbering the Democrats.

re: Editorial, "A New Defense of Voting Rights," July 28, 2013.

Attorney General Eric Holder Jr. is right to seek, through Section 3 of the 1965 Voting Rights Act, some remedy from the Roberts court's and the Republicans' attempt to suppress minority and other voters. However, Mr. Holder has apparently not yet invoked the "liberty" of Fourteenth Amendment's due process clause. This "liberty" over many decades has been used to extend to the states virtually all the rights of the Bill of Rights (which, itself, restricts only the federal government). If "liberty" includes, for example, the right to a lawyer or a trial by jury in criminal cases, how could it not cover the more basic right of the right to vote. This failure to invoke the Fourteenth Amendment is little short of astounding.

War On Women

re: Nick Confessore and Maggie Haberman, "Trump Remains Defiant on News Programs Amid G.O.P. Backlash," 8-10-15

My, oh my, oh my, how outraged are the Republicans about Donald Trump's nasty words about women. On the other hand, devastating women's lives is a-one OK. Deny them health protection offered by Planned Parenthood, including treatment for STDs and cancer screening: a-one OK. Deny them contraception so that they can get unwanted pregnancies: a-one OK. Forbid them abortion of unwanted pregnancies: a-one OK. Insulting women (publicly), that's intolerable; but wrecking their lives: why, that's double a-one OK!

re: Jackie Calmes, "With Two Videos, Activist Ignites Abortion Issue," July 22, 2015.
Editorial, "An Ugly Campaign of Deception," July 22, 2015.

Antiabortion video provocateur, David Daleiden, is continuing his dishonest campaign to malign Planned Parenthood. He's claiming Planned Parenthood makes profits from aborted fetuses' tissues used for medical research—which is an outright lie. It's interesting how these antiabortion zealots are contributing to more abortions by trying to wipe out the most effective prevention of abortion, contraception, which Planned Parenthood provides. About half of the 6.6 million yearly pregnancies in the United States are unintended. They resulted in over 1 million abortions (in 2011). So what these phony "pro-life" zealots are doing by attacking family planning is making sure that there will be hundreds of thousands more abortions, which they view as murders. So the question is, how many more "murders" will it take to satisfy them?

re: Erik Eckholm, "Texas Ruling on Abortion Leads to Call for Clarity," June 11, 2015.
Gail Collins, "Battle of The Abortion Decisions," June 11, 2015.
Editorial, "Closing Off Abortion Rights," June 11, 2015.

Texas wants to deprive women of access to abortion. It claims to being "pro-life"—which it isn't, by all noncontroversial, basic life requirements. Also, supposedly, it wants to help women's health by requiring abortion clinics to have the same (unneeded) facilities as hospitals—this, after trying to decimate Planned Parenthood's cancer screening programs for women. The federal district judge who struck down these restrictions saw right through the hypocrisy and struck down the law, which had so far whittled down abortion clinics in Texas from forty-one to eighteen. A rightist court of appeals, however, upheld the law, which is likely to further reduce these clinics to barely ten. Aside from being an obvious violation of constitutional abortion rights, the law is also a violation of the Fourteenth Amendment's "equal protection of the laws" clause, because only poorer women will be affected; wealthy women can always travel to a more civilized state. It's Texas's poll tax on health.

re: Frances Robles, "With Flurry of Bills, Republican Legislatures Make Abortions Harder to Get," May 10, 2015.

In the last four years, over 200 laws restricting abortion rights have been enacted by state Republicans. Hundreds more are being proposed. They vary from instituting mandatory waiting periods lasting up to 72 hours, to requiring minors to have notarized permissions from their parents, banning abortions after

20 weeks, or compelling abortion doctors to lie to their patients, etc. Bad as these restrictions are, what makes them worse is their too often ignored context. The war on women is related to the war on labor unions (bulwarks of democracy), and to unleashing big money to control the political system under the guise of free speech. All of these point to the same objective: the destruction of democracy. As the Catholic hierarchy/theocracy or various Muslim countries demonstrate, stripping women of rights is necessary for nondemocratic systems. Similarly, they're necessary for establishing an oligarchy here. Time to beware!

re: Jeremy Alford and Erik Eckholm, "With New Bill, Abortion Limits Grow in South," May 22, 2014.

Two scholars, Martin Gilens of Princeton and Benjamin Page of Northwestern University, have provided empirical evidence that we are becoming an oligarchy. Oligarchies have fewer rights than democracies. This helps explain the attack on women's right to abortion that is sweeping much of the country, especially in the South, where the emerging favorite tactic is to require abortion doctors to obtain admitting privileges at adjoining hospitals. Governor Bobby Jindal calls this restriction "a common sense bill that gives women the health and safety protections they deserve." If you believe Hitler loved the Jews, you'll believe Governor Jindal. In a democracy, women own their own bodies, but not so in an oligarchy. The courts will decide whether these restrictions constitute an "undue burden" on women, as if they could be anything else.

re: Gail Collins, "And Now, Political Virgins," April 4, 2015.
Timothy Egan, "Conscience of a Corporation," April 4, 2015.
Editorial, "Big Business and Anti-Gay Laws," April 4, 2015.

The imposing array of big businesses that compelled the socially rightist Republicans in Indiana and Arkansas to quickly abandon their prodiscrimination ("religious rights") laws [protecting businesses who won't serve gay couples] shows where the real muscle of the Republicans lie. Usually, the two—the business Republicans and the socially rightist ones support each other. The first have the money, the second the votes. But LGBT bashing is bad for business, and business comes first. However, like the rightist Roberts Supreme Court, the benevolence toward gays is in contrast to the war on women, which unites the party wings. The likely reason is that LGBT rights don't threaten the primacy of big money, whereas women's rights do. Wherever these rights are strong, democracy thrives, which is just what the Roberts court and Republicans don't want. This accords with their war on labor and voter suppression.

re: Editorial, "A Perilous Year for Abortion Rights," January 20, 2015.

There are two widespread myths about abortion. First, that abortion opponents are "pro-life," which would be true only if life ended at birth. The pro-life positions of the antichoice people are pathetic on real, undisputed causes of death: poverty, malnutrition, disease, lack of health care, wars, and ecological disasters. The pro-choice people have much better track records on these real issues. Secondly, that there is a general war on abortion. There is only a war on poor women having abortions, not rich women. Wealthy women can always travel to a more civilized state or nation to get whatever abortions they want. It's poor women who are restricted by the war on abortion. The real issue is whether only wealthy women, rather than all women, should have the right to abortion.

re: Nicholas Kristof, "Politicians, Teens, and Birth Control," November 13, 2014.

Nicholas Kristof reports interesting data: Some one-third of teenage girls become pregnant—three times Spain's rate, five times France's, and fifteen times Switzerland's. A major reason for these discrepancies is that we don't adequately finance education on sex and pregnancy. Medicaid spends nearly thirteen thousand dollars per birth, but only eight dollars (!) per teenager on pregnancy education. LARCs (IUDs) are much more effective than condoms, but the initial cost ranges from five hundred to one thousand dollars, something many youths cannot afford. A Saint Louis study indicated that free distribution of IUDs reduced pregnancy rates by three-quarters. Each one of these figures feature Republicans as the guilty party, whether opposing family planning, sex education, or affordable care governmentally funded. They illustrate the utter hypocrisy of most antichoice people (so-called "pro-life") who much prefer condemning abortions than preventing pregnancies.

re: Erik Eckholm, "Access to Abortion Falling as States Pass Restrictions," January 4, 2014.

Abortion, Democracy, and Slavery

Citing the Guttmacher Institute, Erik Eckholm notes that numerous states are shredding the right to abortion. In the last three years, over 200 restrictive measures have been passed by thirty states. Rationales have included protecting women "from the harms" of abortion (but not the harm of unwanted children) to preventing the "fetal pain" refuted by major medical groups. That these rightists should lament the alleged pain of the unborn while ignoring the pain of the living, indeed, even inflicting such pains on the unemployed, the weak, and the poor, is scandalous. These attacks on basic democratic liberties is conjoined to attacking labor unions (one of the few and waning checks on corporate and financial power), and trying to strip the votes from millions of minorities—thereby repudiating the essence of democracy, universal suffrage. Even worse is telling women that, in matters of procreation, they don't own their own bodies, the states (like Texas) do. But that's the definition of slavery, when your body belongs to another, which fits with the revival of the Confederate flag among these groups. It's time to wake up to the danger of these rightist extremists, before we find ourselves completely enmeshed in fascism.

re: Marina Villeneuve, "Helping to Fund Abortions," August 26, 2013.

Do Only Wealthy Women Have the Right to Abortions?

Marina Villeneuve reports that 42 percent of women having abortions have an income below the poverty line. These are the women the Republicans expect won't be able to get abortions because of various onerous requirements, like waiting periods (obliging them to make two trips), having to pay for mandatory ultrasounds, and shutting down nearby clinics (compelling longer and more expensive trips and more time off work). These facts require that we reexamine the abortion issue. It's not just about whether women should have the right to their own bodies, but also, do only wealthy women have the right to an abortion? That's because wealthy women living in a reactionary or authoritarian state can easily move to a more civilized state or country and exercise their procreative rights. That option is not open to poor women.

Erik Eckholm, "Theory on Pain Is Driving Rules for Abortions," August 2, 2013.

The rightists/Republicans—led by Mary Balch's professed horror at the alleged pain (debunked by the scientific community) suffered by the fetus—have succeeded in a dozen states to enact laws banning abortions after twenty weeks. These same rightists/Republicans don't show the least concern for the very real pain of those living on minimum wages (whose hike they oppose) with what that means for adequate food or housing; or for those who cannot afford health insurance and effective medical care; or for women on whom they would force unwanted children; or for minorities, whose votes they seek to suppress; or for the needy, whose food stamps they want to reduce. But my, oh my, oh my, how deeply, deeply they feel the pain of the unborn. Their professed concern would be hilarious, were it not an ominous part of their war on women.

re: Jeremy W. Peters, "In Partisan Vote, House Approves Ban on Abortions after Twenty-Two Weeks," June 19, 2013.

For years, the war on women has relied on the phony "pro-life" rationalizations by bigots who seem to believe that life begins at conception and ends at birth. Don't expect any life-support or any "pro-life" actions on behalf of poor children and mothers from that gang. Now, they've come up with a new rationale—that fetuses feel pain and they just can't put up with these "atrocities against the babies." No problem putting up with the atrocities of being underfed, of brain development arrested because of poverty, of not having your parents present because they're forced to work at odd and unpredictable hours, of hunger that cripples learning at school, or living in neighborhoods filled with crime, drugs, poverty, unemployment, and fear. Don't expect these hypocrites ever to be concerned with that kind of "atrocity."

re: Editorial, "Courage in Kansas," April 14, 2013.

The violent, even murderous, "pro-life" pretenders have already killed several brave abortion providers, including Dr. George Tiller in Wichita, Kansas, whose clinic was shut down. Courageous providers and colleagues are trying to reopen a clinic in Wichita and are facing legal battles and renewed threats of violence. The murderers, and those who encourage them, pretend to be pro-life, but what that means in practice is that life begins at conception and ends at birth, since they typically oppose provisions that help poor mothers take care of their children. The best way to prevent abortions is to practice family planning and contraception, which the pro-life haters condemn. Their proclivity for violence is matched only by their dishonesty and false piety.

rc: Jonathan Weisman, "Rape Remark Jolts a Senate Race, and the Presidential One, Too," October 25, 2012.

When Todd Akin talked about "legitimate rape," prominent Republicans couldn't run away fast enough. Now Indiana Senate contender Richard Mourdock sees a rapist getting a woman pregnant to be what "God intended," and Republicans are also running from that. What they find so scary about Akin and Mourdock is that the public will learn the truth about the real face of the Republican Party. The views of most Republicans, including Paul Ryan's, are virtually identical to Akin's and Mourdock's. As for Romney's public support of the "personhood" amendment that would criminalize all abortions, that puts him on board, whatever his later strategic denials claim. The Republican Party is antiwomen—witness the multitude of bills they have proposed statewide and nationwide to strip women of abortion, contraception, health care, and equal pay options—but cannot afford to be seen that way. This is why Mourdock produces their latest discomfiture.

Morally Responsible for Dr. Tiller's Murder: the Media's Use of "Pro-Life"

The Justice Department will investigate if others besides Scott Roeder were involved in the murder of Dr. George Tiller ("Killing of Kansas Doctor Becomes a Federal Case, Too," June 6, 2009). However, it will not and cannot investigate those having some moral responsibility for such murders. The latter would include the media who have irresponsibly adopted the self-awarded label of "pro-life," monopolized by the antichoice movements and politicians. Yet this label is demonstrably false if we look at the track record of these antichoice leaders on the real, basic pro-life issues: (1) malnutrition, famine, physical hardships, poverty, (2) diseases, poor health, lack of medical care, (3) ecological dislocations and disasters, and (4) deathly violence, especially from militarism and war. On all these issues, the pro-life people are overwhelmingly the pro-choice people, and vice-versa. This can be easily checked by, for example, analyzing the voting records of US representatives and senators. Of course, some antichoice leaders are truly pro-life, but not nearly in the majority that pro-choice supporters are.

Yet the media continue using the misnomer "pro-life," thereby serving to justify the demented fanatics who murder "baby-killers." It's more than overdue to strip right-wing zealots of their undeserved "pro-life" mantle. The media are not criminally responsible for the harassment, violence, and murders against abortion supporters and providers. But their moral complicity is undeniable and must stop.

Conclusion

THERE HAS LONG BEEN A dichotomy between American ideals and our actions. The latter have been too often imperialistic and anti-democratic, whereas our official values are democratic, egalitarian, and anti-colonial. America is at a crossroad. Should we try to recapture the democratic elements of our society which have been more recently compromised, or should we just tremblingly adjust to the new oligarchic realities?

The demise of elements of democracy is due not only to economic structures and the power of the oligarchs, but also due to unwholesome public ignorance of what is really happening in our society and abroad. These letters are an attempt to decrease this ignorance and encourage our commitment to real democracy, and not one in name only.

My efforts are part of a broader movement that includes Hispanics, Blacks, Progressives, women, and labor unions. We all seek a more humane capitalism — it was once possible under the New Deal. Whether it's possible again, only time will tell. It may require a collapse before this new global financial capitalism can be changed, either toward greater fascism or toward socialism. On the other hand, the huge crowds being drawn by social-democratic presidential candidate, Bernie Sanders, is a sign of encouragement. People across the political spectrum suffer and want change. Will they be brainwashed or beguiled, once again, to elect those politicians blocking change, while falsely pretending to want it? We'll see.

Appendix

I. BACKGROUND—DOMESTIC—A VERY BRIEF ECONOMIC HISTORY

IN THE LAST FIFTY YEARS, the United States has witnessed a huge transfer of wealth from the poor and middle classes to the upper 1 percent, or one-tenth of 1 percent. The share of the national household wealth held by the top 0.1 percent (not 1 percent but 0.1 percent) jumped from 7 percent in the 1970s to 22 percent today.

The Forbes 400 first appeared in 1982. Thirty-six members of the debut issue were still in the Forbes 400 in 2012, but with bloated wealth: Stephen Bechtel from $200 million to $2.9 billion in 2012; Warren Buffett, from $250 million to $40 billion; Ray Lee Hunt, $200 million to $5.2 billion are some examples.

Kevin Phillips (*Wealth and Democracy*) charted the ratio between the richest family and the median family income: it was 10,000:1 in 1803; 138,000:1 in 1962; and 1,416,000:1 in 1999. In 2014, Forbes reported the Walton family as worth nearly $150 billion, while two Koch brothers were worth $42 billion each. The Forbes 400 richest totaled $2.29 trillion in 2014, which, Senator Bernie Sanders (Vermont) noted, constituted more wealth than the bottom half of America.

As the rich got wealthier, workers got poorer, partly because of the drastic weakening of labor unions through technology and globalization. Union membership shrank from nearly one-third of all workers in 1960 to 11.1 percent in 2014.

Median family income declined by almost five thousand dollars since 1999—while the twenty-five highest-earning hedge fund managers and traders averaged an income of one billion dollars each in 2013. In 1980, the top CEOs earned forty-two times what workers earned; by 2013, this had mushroomed to some 300:1.

The huge discrepancies in wealth affected politics. The 2012 elections cost some seven billion dollars. Labor was outspent 15:1 by business. Furthermore, the rightist Roberts Supreme Court has allowed virtually unlimited big (and even secret) money to corrupt elections. Thus, the Koch brothers–backed network announced its intention to spend $889 million in the 2016 presidential race.

The power of big money is reflected in tax policy. Corporate taxes represented 28 percent of federal revenues in the 1950s. By the 2000s, this had shrunk to 7 percent. This was compensated by a sharp rise of individual income taxes (rising from 58 percent of federal revenues in the 1950s to over 80 percent by 2012), thereby shifting the burden to the less-favored classes. Similarly, the highest marginal individual income tax rates also shrank from 90 percent in the 1950s to 39 percent today.

The increasing polarization in wealth included a declining middle class, while turning the United States into an oligarchy. A paper by Princeton professor Martin Gilens and Northwestern University professor Benjamin I. Page ("Testing Theories of American Politics: Elites, Interest Groups, and Average Citizens," in *Perspective on Politics*, September 2014) studied 1,779 policy issues and found the outcome overwhelmingly favorable to elites, "while average citizens and mass-based interest groups have little or no independent influence."

While not using the term, the paper clearly indicated the oligarchic nature of our society. French economist Thomas Piketty made quite a splash in 2014 with his book *Capital in the Twenty-First Century*. He also saw the growth of oligarchy: oligarchic divergence—"a process in which the rich countries would come to be owned by their own billionaires or, more generally, in which all countries... would come to be owned more and more by the planet's billionaires and multi-millionaires. As noted, this process is already well under way."

One expression of this is the alienation of the public toward the major political institutions. A Gallup poll in June 2014 showed that only 7 percent of Americans have "a great deal" or "quite a lot" of confidence in Congress, only 29 percent for the presidency, and 30 percent for the Supreme Court—21 percent for big business.

These are the salient essentially economic data of the last fifty years.

II. BACKGROUND—FOREIGN POLICY

US history is the history of expanding imperialism. It started with the Indians, whose population plummeted by 70 percent by 1900, before rising again. John O'Sullivan's 1845 phrase of "manifest destiny to overspread the continent" meant that Mexico was next. It lost over half its territory to the United States following its defeat and the 1848 Treaty of Guadalupe Hidalgo.

Having spanned the continent, the United States then turned its expansion overseas. Victory over Spain in the 1898 Spanish-American War led to the occupation of Cuba, Puerto Rico, and the Philippines, the gateway to Asia.

In 1895, Secretary of State Richard Olney boasted, "Today, the United States is practically sovereign on this continent and its fiat is law." This was followed by taking Panama from Colombia in 1903 and the Theodore Roosevelt Corollary of 1904 that claimed for the United States the right to an international police power anywhere in the hemisphere. This was followed by numerous interventions—typically to establish dictatorships there.

World War I gave the United States the opportunity for the first time to intervene in European affairs when France, England, and Russia were too weak to defeat Kaiser Germany without American help. Woodrow Wilson also sent troops to Russia to try to defeat the Bolshevik Revolution, an aggression that was shared by a dozen other countries, including France and England.

World War II extended American influence in Europe. When Harry S. Truman became president in 1945, he was informed of the atomic bomb project. If the bomb worked, Truman said, "I'll certainly have a hammer on those boys," alluding to the Russians.

The defeat of the Axis meant the defeat of forms of capitalism. Socialism seemed to many to offer a better answer. It was the task of the United States, as the foremost global capitalist power, to make sure that neither socialism nor communism would spread. Already in 1941, Henry Luce, publisher of *Life*, *TIME*, and *Fortune* opined that "the American Century" had dawned and we would dominate the world. American foreign policy became anchored in preventing Soviet expansion, although it was the United States that in fact was expanding globally.

In 1947, the Truman Doctrine asserted the right of the United States to intervene anywhere globally to suppress revolution. The United States also questioned the Soviet right to have friendly regimes on its borders. The CIA was busy at work trying to destroy leftist regimes—for example, Patrice Lumumba in the Congo, Arbenz in Guatemala (1954), Castro in Cuba (1960), Allende in Chile (1973), or the Sandinistas in Nicaragua (1980s), regardless of whether they had been democratically supported/elected. The United States had deployed hundreds of bases throughout the world and accounted by itself for nearly half of the whole world's military expenditures according to SIPRI (Stockholm International Peace Research Institute). Its hegemony seemed assured by the collapse of the Soviet Union in 1990–1991. It had its corrupt and incompetent puppet, Boris Yeltsin, preside over a truncated Russia from 1991 to 1999.

But things were not all that promising. Yeltsin was succeeded by Vladimir Putin in 2000, and China had a mushrooming economy. American industry, which had been supreme throughout the previous century, began a sharp decline through globalization and the new primacy of a financial oligarchy.

In 1998, the United States decided to expand NATO eastward to Hungary, Poland, and the Czech Republic, despite its promise to Soviet President Mikhail Gorbachev that it would not do so. More former Soviet countries were incorporated, including the Baltic Republics on Russia's doorstep. George F. Kennan had warned this NATO expansion was a "tragic mistake" that would start a new Cold War. His words were unfortunately prophetic when, fearing the Ukraine would be the next NATO member, President Putin in 2014 unleashed Russian forces in eastern Ukraine, pretty much as Kennan had predicted.

In the meantime, the US 2003 invasion of Iraq and subsequent occupation unleashed a catastrophic chain of events that led to disintegrating societies in Libya, Yemen, Syria, and elsewhere, and a rise of terrorism spearheaded by ISIS (ISIL, Islamic State). America's enormous military capacity seemed stymied by these events. Its economy suffered from neglect of domestic needs in order to feed huge military expenditures in the trillions.

As of this writing, American leaders are pondering whether economic sanctions on Russia are insufficient and need to be supplemented by heavily arming the Ukrainians. Our goal remains global supremacy, but it brings up the question whether our resources will continue to be adequate for this global hegemony.

Made in the USA
San Bernardino, CA
27 November 2015